DOCTOR STRANGE VOL. 5: SECRET EMPIRE. Contains material originally published in magazine form as DOCTOR STRANGE #21-26. First printing 2017. ISBN 978-1-302-90589-7. Published by MARVEL WORLDWIDE, INC., a subsidiary of MARVEL ENTERTAINMENT, LLC. OFFICE OF PUBLICATION: 135 West 50th Street, New York, NY 10020. Copyright © 2017 MARVEL No similarity between any of the names, characters, persons, and/or institutions in this magazine with those of any living or dead person or institution is intended, and any such similarity which may exist is purely coincidental. **Printed in the U.S.A.** DAN BUCKLEY, President, Marvel Entertainment; JOE QUESADA, Chief Creative Officer; TOM BREVOORT, SVP of Publishing; DAVID BOGART, SVP of Business Affairs & Operations, Publishing & Partnership; C.B. CEBULSKI, VP of Brand Management & Development, Asia; DAVID GABRIEL, SVP of Sales & Marketing, Publishing; JEFF YOUNGQUIST, VP of Production & Special Projects; DAN CARR, Executive Director of Publishing Technology; ALEX MORALES, Director of Publishing Operations; SUSAN CRESPI, Production Manager; STAN LEE, Chairman Emeritus. For information regarding advertising in Marvel Comics or on Marvel.com, please contact Jonathan Parkhideh, VP of Digital Media & Marketing Solutions, at jparkhideh@marvel.com. For Marvel subscription inquiries, please call 888-511-5480. **Manufactured between 11/17/2017 and 12/18/2017 by LSC COMMUNICATIONS INC., KENDALLVILLE, IN, USA.**

10 9 8 7 6 5 4 3 2 1

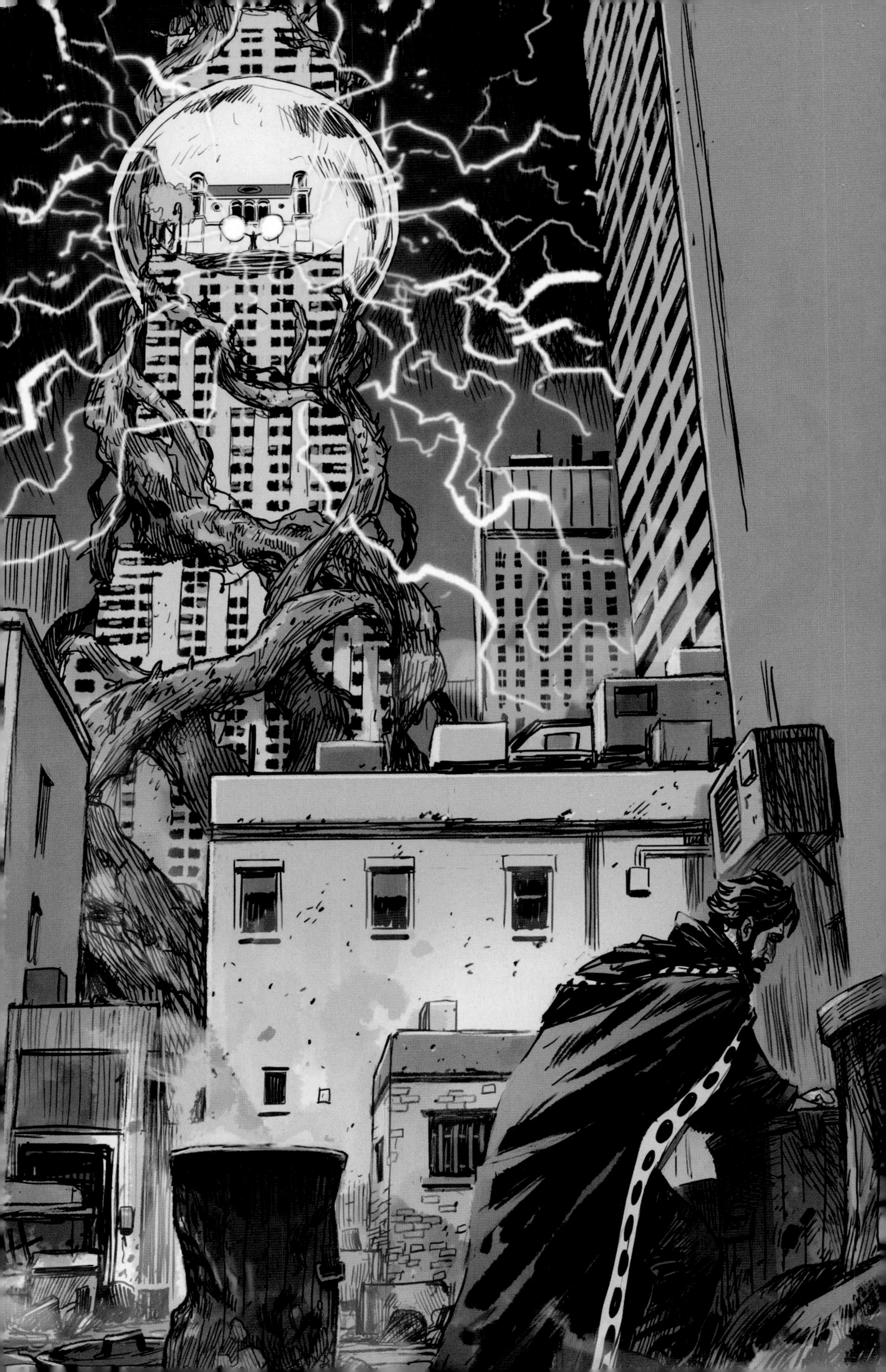

DOCTOR STRANGE

Secret Empire

ISSUES #21-24

Dennis Hopeless
WRITER

Niko Henrichon
ARTIST/COLORIST

CHRIS BACHALO & TIM TOWNSEND WITH JAVA TARTAGLIA (#21) COVER ART, #21-22
NIKO HENRICHON COVER ART, #23-24

ISSUE #25

John Barber
WRITER

*Kevin Nowlan, Scott Hanna, Dexter Vines, Mark Morales,
Terry Pallot, Tom Palmer & Dan Brown*
PAST SEQUENCE ART

Juan Frigeri & Java Tartaglia
PRESENT SEQUENCE ART

KEVIN NOWLAN COVER ART

ISSUES #26

John Barber
WRITER

Niko Henrichon
ARTIST/COLORIST

JAKUB REBELKA COVER ART

VC's CORY PETIT
LETTERER

ALLISON STOCK &
KATHLEEN WISNESKI
ASSISTANT EDITORS

DARREN SHAN
ASSOCIATE EDITOR

NICK LOWE
EDITOR

DOCTOR STRANGE CREATED BY STAN LEE & STEVE DITKO

COLLECTION EDITOR: JENNIFER GRÜNWALD
ASSISTANT EDITOR: CAITLIN O'CONNELL
ASSOCIATE MANAGING EDITOR: KATERI WOODY
EDITOR, SPECIAL PROJECTS: MARK D. BEAZLEY
VP PRODUCTION & SPECIAL PROJECTS: JEFF YOUNGQUIST
SVP PRINT, SALES & MARKETING: DAVID GABRIEL
BOOK DESIGNER: JAY BOWEN

EDITOR IN CHIEF: AXEL ALONSO
CHIEF CREATIVE OFFICER: JOE QUESADA
PRESIDENT: DAN BUCKLEY
EXECUTIVE PRODUCER: ALAN FINE

STEPHEN STRANGE WAS A PREEMINENT SURGEON UNTIL A CAR ACCIDENT
DAMAGED THE NERVES IN HIS HANDS. HIS EGO DROVE HIM TO SCOUR THE
GLOBE FOR A MIRACLE CURE, BUT INSTEAD HE FOUND A MYSTERIOUS WIZARD
CALLED THE ANCIENT ONE WHO TAUGHT HIM MAGIC AND THAT THERE ARE
THINGS IN THIS WORLD BIGGER THAN HIMSELF. THESE LESSONS LED STEPHEN
TO BECOME THE SORCERER SUPREME, EARTH'S FIRST DEFENSE AGAINST ALL
MANNER OF MAGICAL THREATS. HIS PATIENTS CALL HIM...

DOCTOR STRANGE

A COSMIC CUBE transformed Steve Rogers, A.K.A.
Captain America, into the ultimate Hydra sleeper agent
— and after months of scheming and manipulation, the
country is now under Hydra's control. Doctor Strange and
some of Earth's street-level heroes are trapped inside the
Darkforce bubble that envelops New York City.

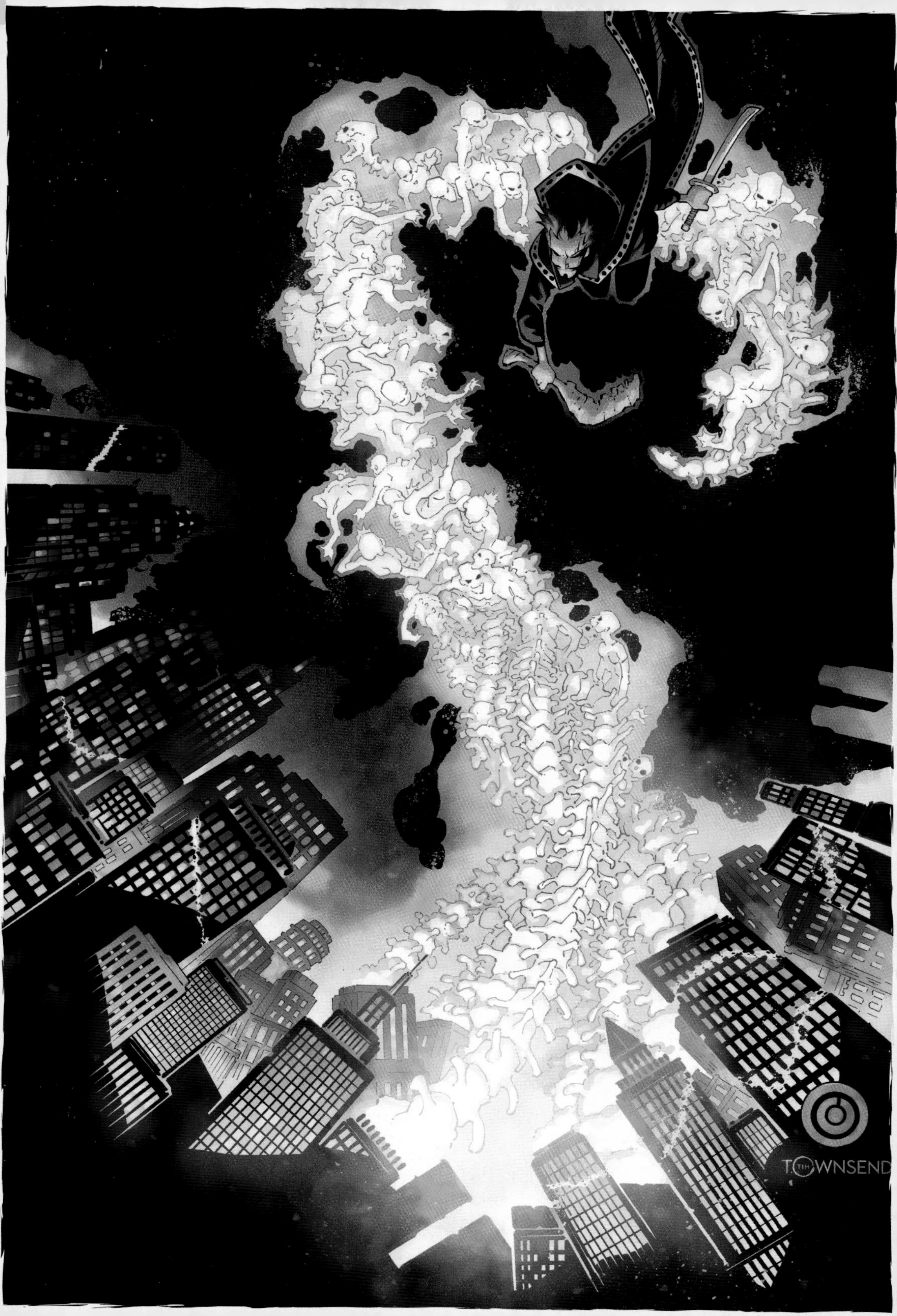
TOWNSEND

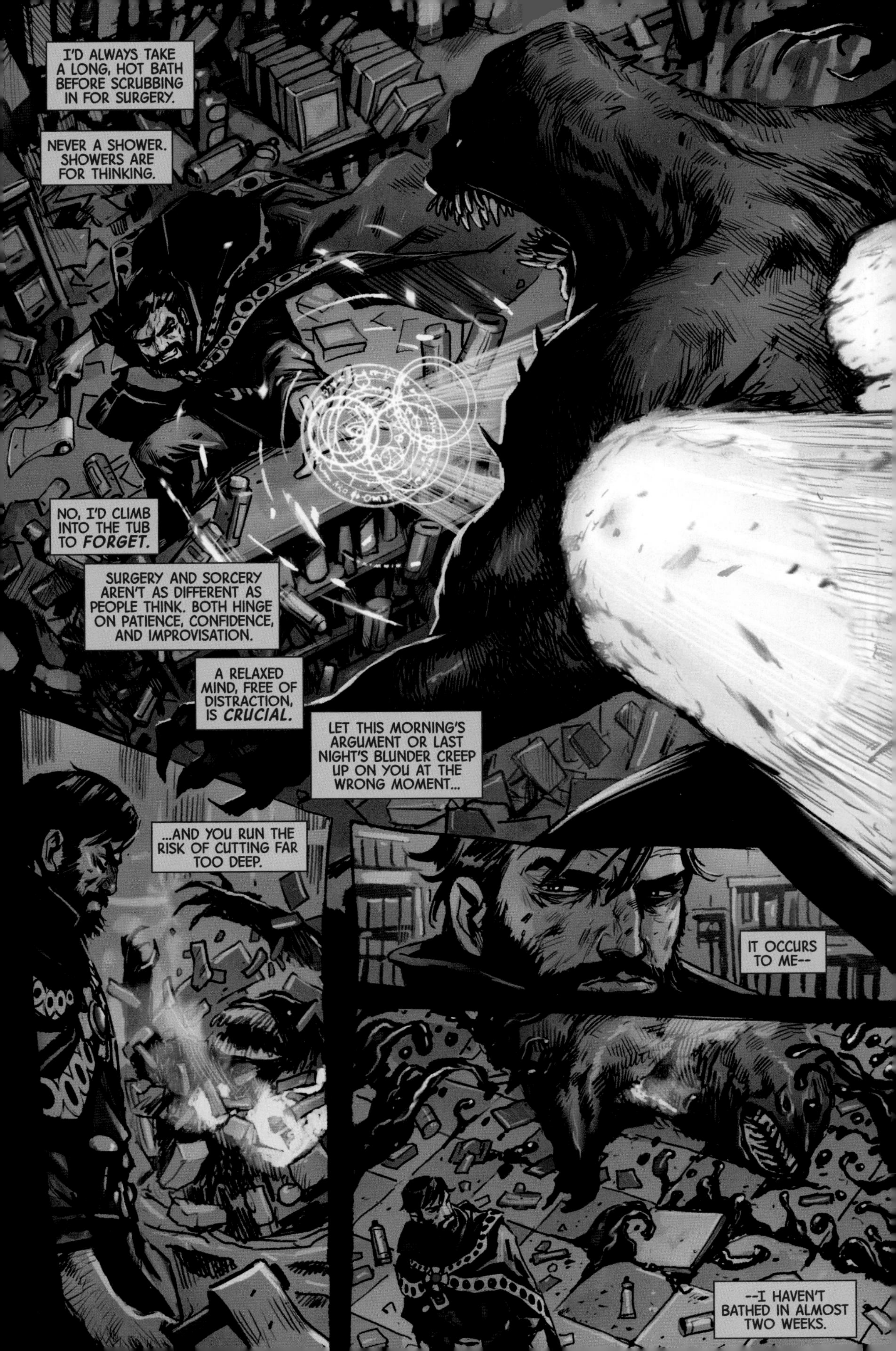
I'D ALWAYS TAKE A LONG, HOT BATH BEFORE SCRUBBING IN FOR SURGERY.
NEVER A SHOWER. SHOWERS ARE FOR THINKING.
NO, I'D CLIMB INTO THE TUB TO *FORGET.*
SURGERY AND SORCERY AREN'T AS DIFFERENT AS PEOPLE THINK. BOTH HINGE ON PATIENCE, CONFIDENCE, AND IMPROVISATION.
A RELAXED MIND, FREE OF DISTRACTION, IS *CRUCIAL.*
LET THIS MORNING'S ARGUMENT OR LAST NIGHT'S BLUNDER CREEP UP ON YOU AT THE WRONG MOMENT...
...AND YOU RUN THE RISK OF CUTTING FAR TOO DEEP.
IT OCCURS TO ME--
--I HAVEN'T BATHED IN ALMOST TWO WEEKS.

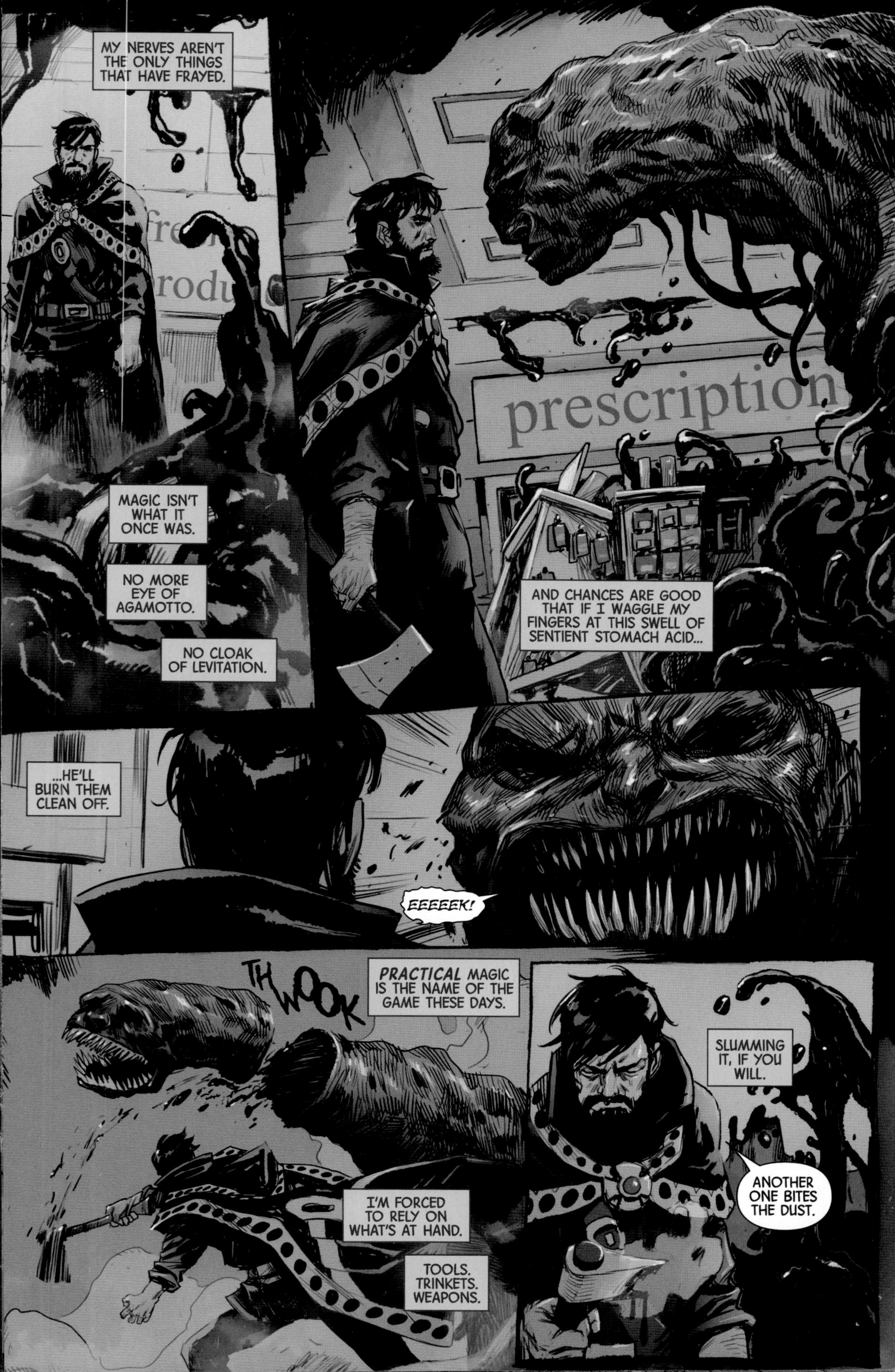
MY NERVES AREN'T THE ONLY THINGS THAT HAVE FRAYED.
fresh produce
prescription
MAGIC ISN'T WHAT IT ONCE WAS.
NO MORE EYE OF AGAMOTTO.
NO CLOAK OF LEVITATION.
AND CHANCES ARE GOOD THAT IF I WAGGLE MY FINGERS AT THIS SWELL OF SENTIENT STOMACH ACID...
...HE'LL BURN THEM CLEAN OFF.
EEEEEK!
THWOOK
PRACTICAL MAGIC IS THE NAME OF THE GAME THESE DAYS.
I'M FORCED TO RELY ON WHAT'S AT HAND.
TOOLS. TRINKETS. WEAPONS.
SLUMMING IT, IF YOU WILL.
ANOTHER ONE BITES THE DUST.

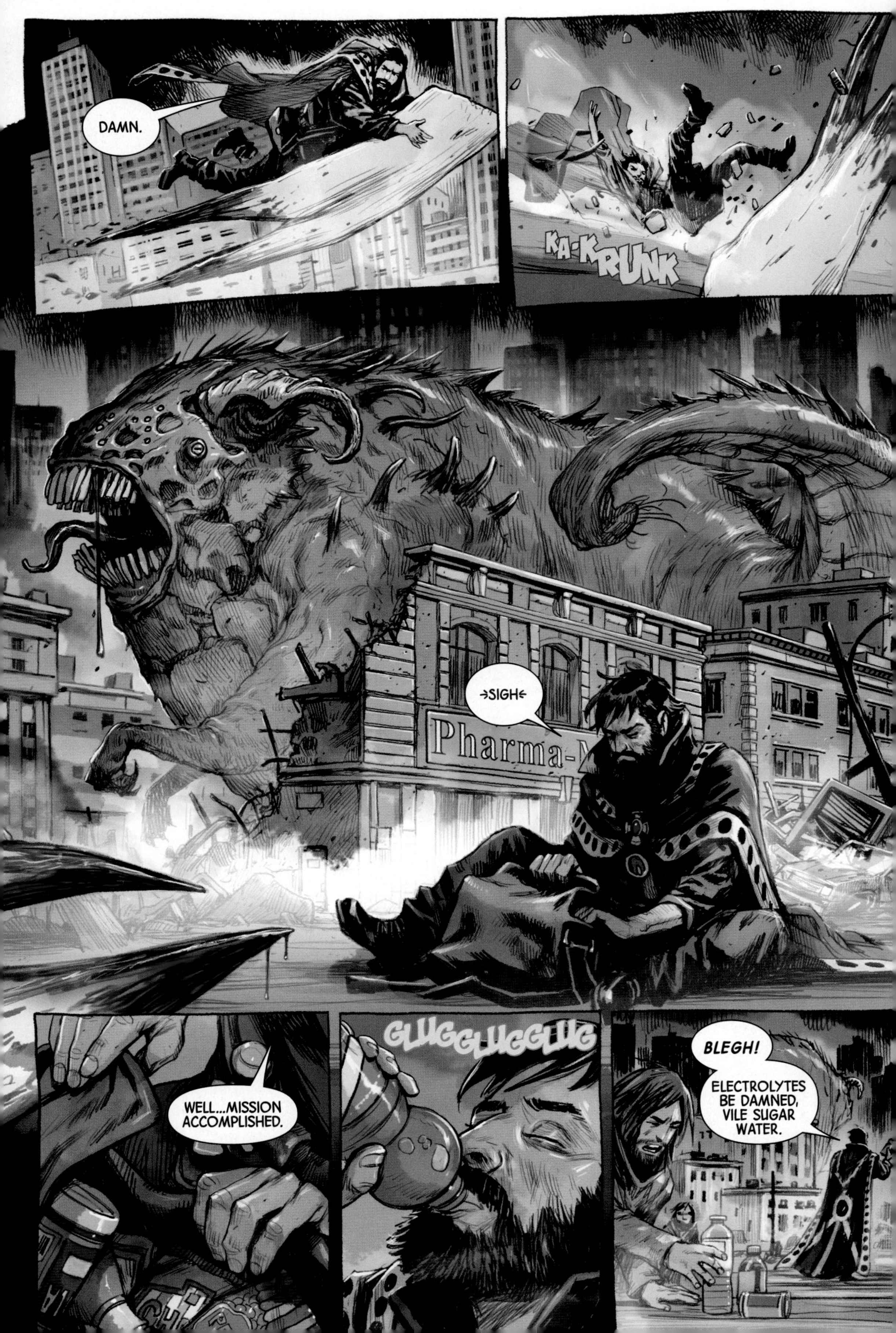
DAMN.
KA-KRUNK
Pharma-M
SIGH
WELL...MISSION ACCOMPLISHED.
GLUGGLUGGLUG
BLEGH!
ELECTROLYTES BE DAMNED, VILE SUGAR WATER.

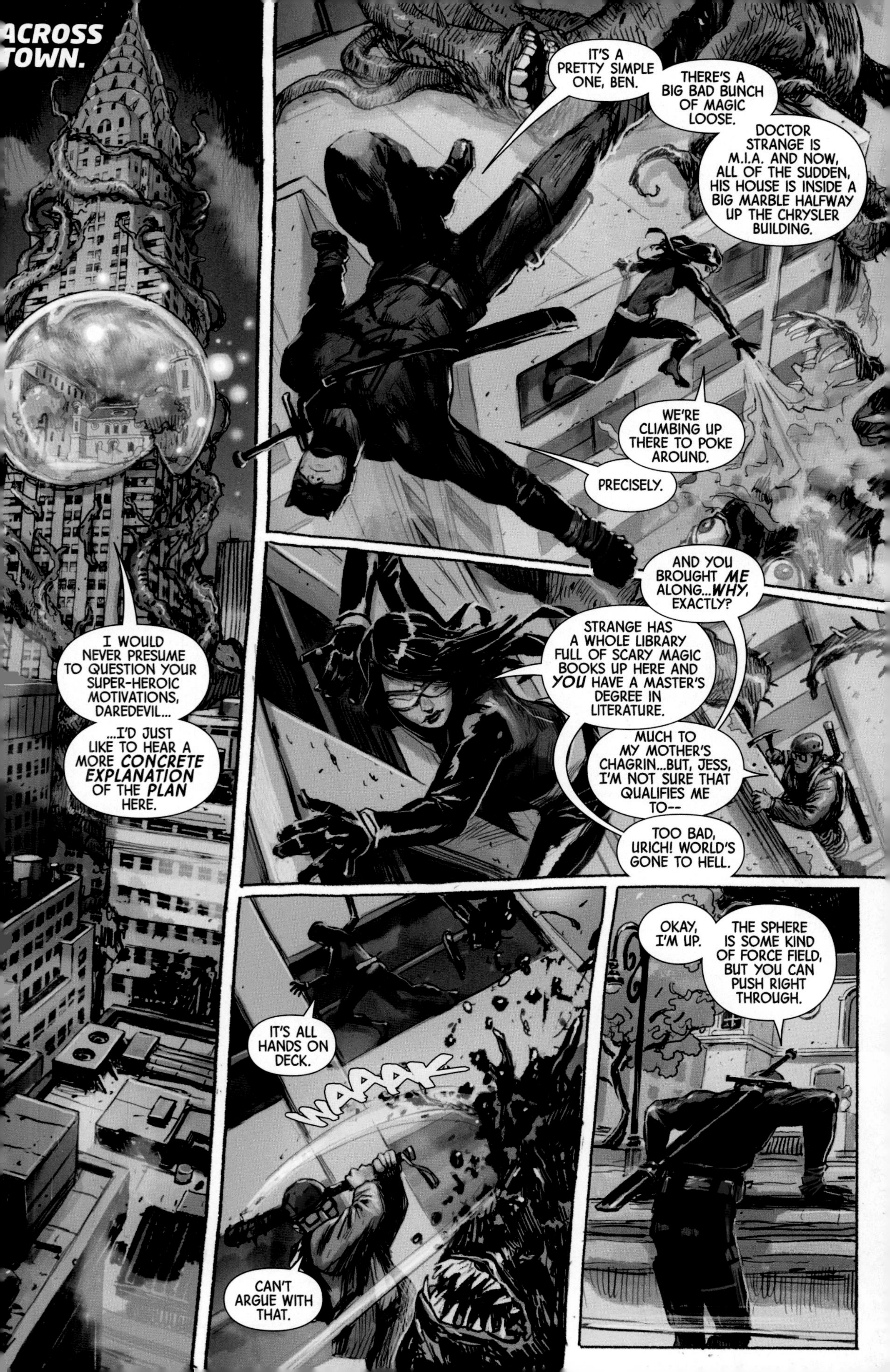
ACROSS TOWN.
IT'S A PRETTY SIMPLE ONE, BEN.
THERE'S A BIG BAD BUNCH OF MAGIC LOOSE.
DOCTOR STRANGE IS M.I.A. AND NOW, ALL OF THE SUDDEN, HIS HOUSE IS INSIDE A BIG MARBLE HALFWAY UP THE CHRYSLER BUILDING.
WE'RE CLIMBING UP THERE TO POKE AROUND.
PRECISELY.
I WOULD NEVER PRESUME TO QUESTION YOUR SUPER-HEROIC MOTIVATIONS, DAREDEVIL...
...I'D JUST LIKE TO HEAR A MORE CONCRETE EXPLANATION OF THE PLAN HERE.
AND YOU BROUGHT ME ALONG...WHY, EXACTLY?
STRANGE HAS A WHOLE LIBRARY FULL OF SCARY MAGIC BOOKS UP HERE AND YOU HAVE A MASTER'S DEGREE IN LITERATURE.
MUCH TO MY MOTHER'S CHAGRIN...BUT, JESS, I'M NOT SURE THAT QUALIFIES ME TO--
TOO BAD, URICH! WORLD'S GONE TO HELL.
IT'S ALL HANDS ON DECK.
WAPPK
CAN'T ARGUE WITH THAT.
OKAY, I'M UP.
THE SPHERE IS SOME KIND OF FORCE FIELD, BUT YOU CAN PUSH RIGHT THROUGH.

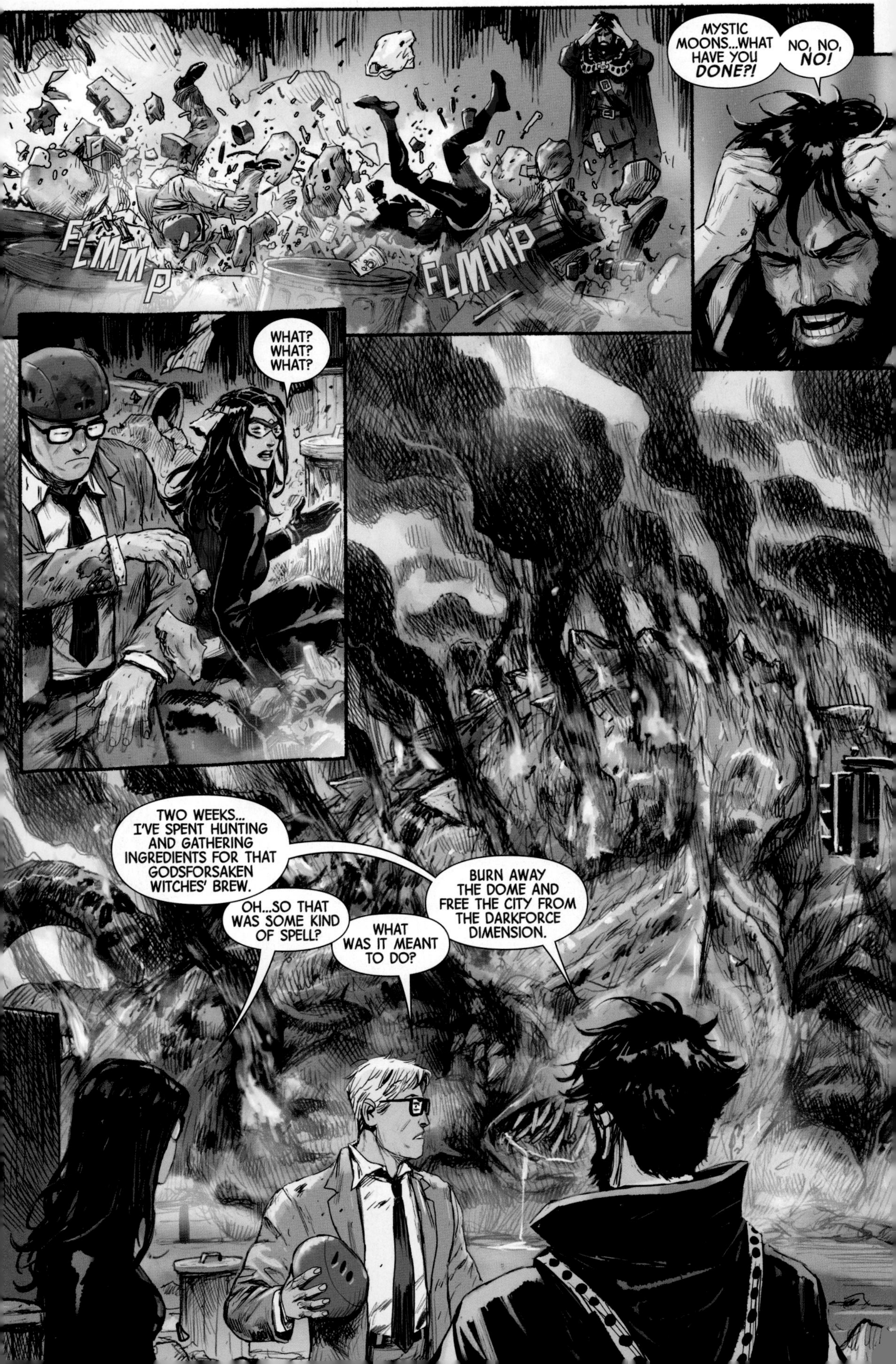
FLMMP
FLMMP
MYSTIC MOONS...WHAT HAVE YOU DONE?!
NO, NO, NO!
WHAT? WHAT? WHAT?
TWO WEEKS... I'VE SPENT HUNTING AND GATHERING INGREDIENTS FOR THAT GODSFORSAKEN WITCHES' BREW.
BURN AWAY THE DOME AND FREE THE CITY FROM THE DARKFORCE DIMENSION.
OH...SO THAT WAS SOME KIND OF SPELL?
WHAT WAS IT MEANT TO DO?

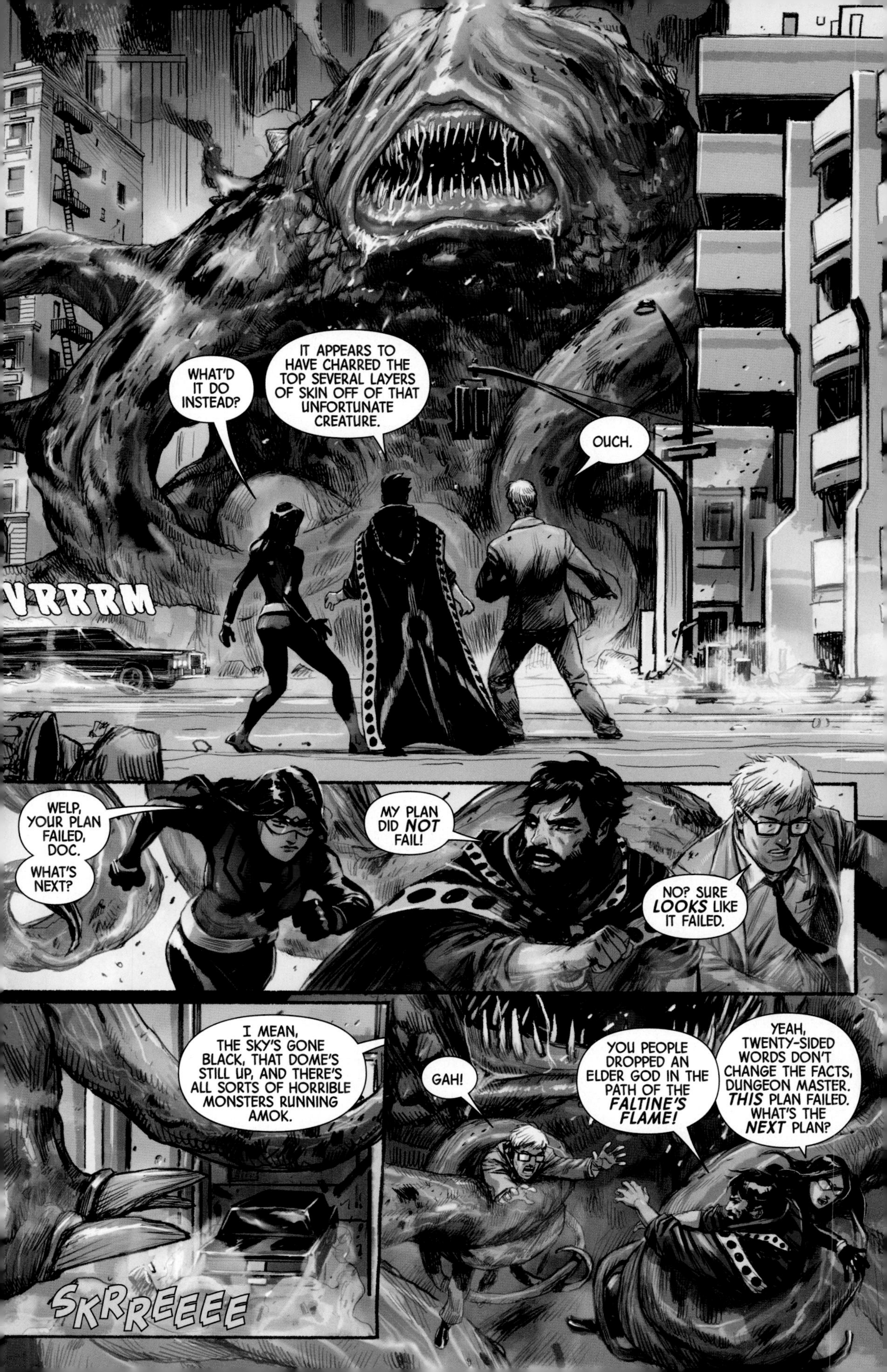
WHAT'D IT DO INSTEAD?
IT APPEARS TO HAVE CHARRED THE TOP SEVERAL LAYERS OF SKIN OFF OF THAT UNFORTUNATE CREATURE.
OUCH.
VRRRM
WELP, YOUR PLAN FAILED, DOC.
WHAT'S NEXT?
MY PLAN DID NOT FAIL!
NO? SURE LOOKS LIKE IT FAILED.
I MEAN, THE SKY'S GONE BLACK, THAT DOME'S STILL UP, AND THERE'S ALL SORTS OF HORRIBLE MONSTERS RUNNING AMOK.
GAH!
YOU PEOPLE DROPPED AN ELDER GOD IN THE PATH OF THE FALTINE'S FLAME!
YEAH, TWENTY-SIDED WORDS DON'T CHANGE THE FACTS, DUNGEON MASTER. THIS PLAN FAILED. WHAT'S THE NEXT PLAN?
SKRREEEE

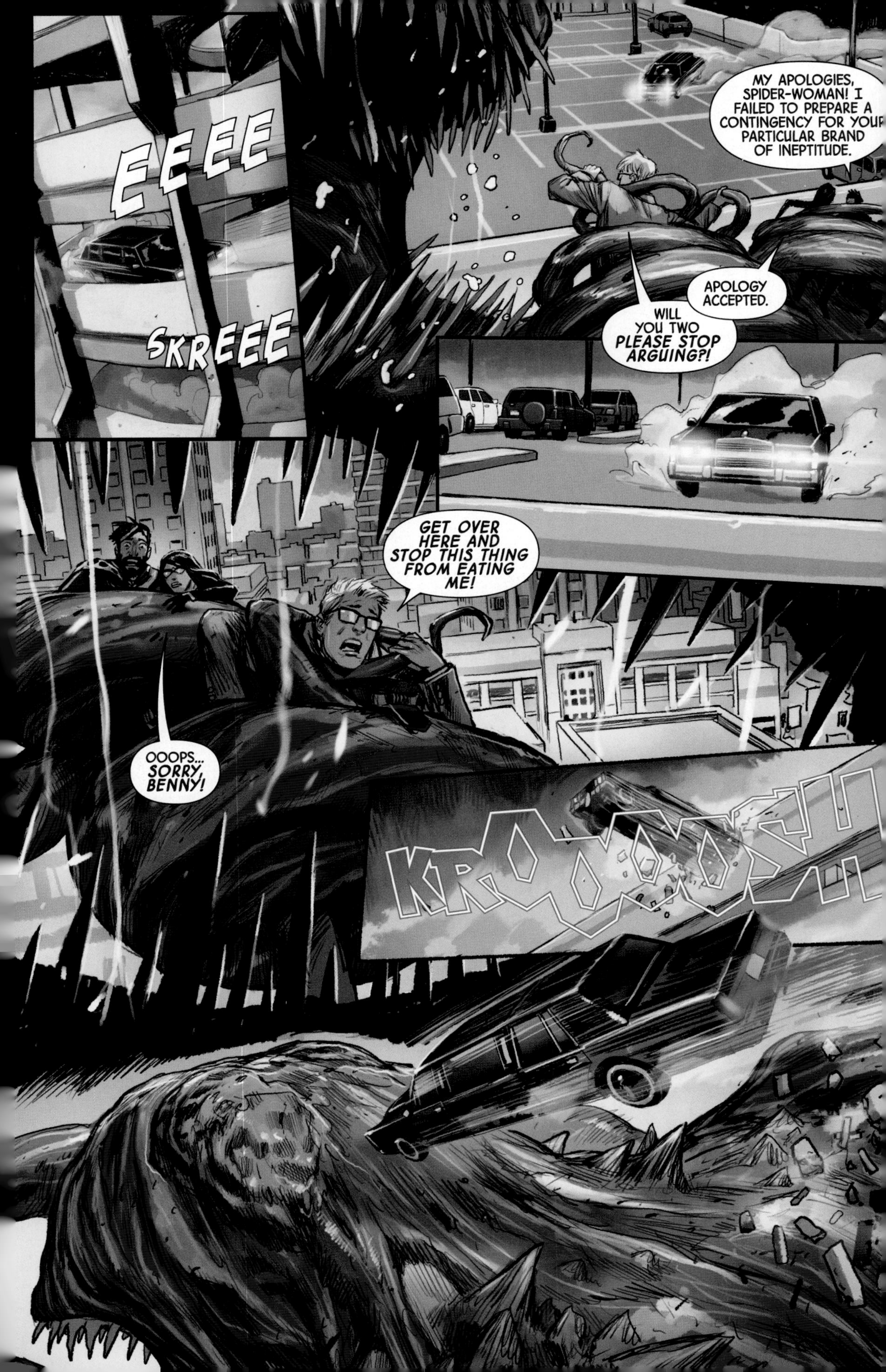
EEEE
SKREEE
MY APOLOGIES, SPIDER-WOMAN! I FAILED TO PREPARE A CONTINGENCY FOR YOUR PARTICULAR BRAND OF INEPTITUDE.
APOLOGY ACCEPTED.
WILL YOU TWO PLEASE STOP ARGUING?!
GET OVER HERE AND STOP THIS THING FROM EATING ME!
OOOPS... SORRY, BENNY!
KROOOOSH

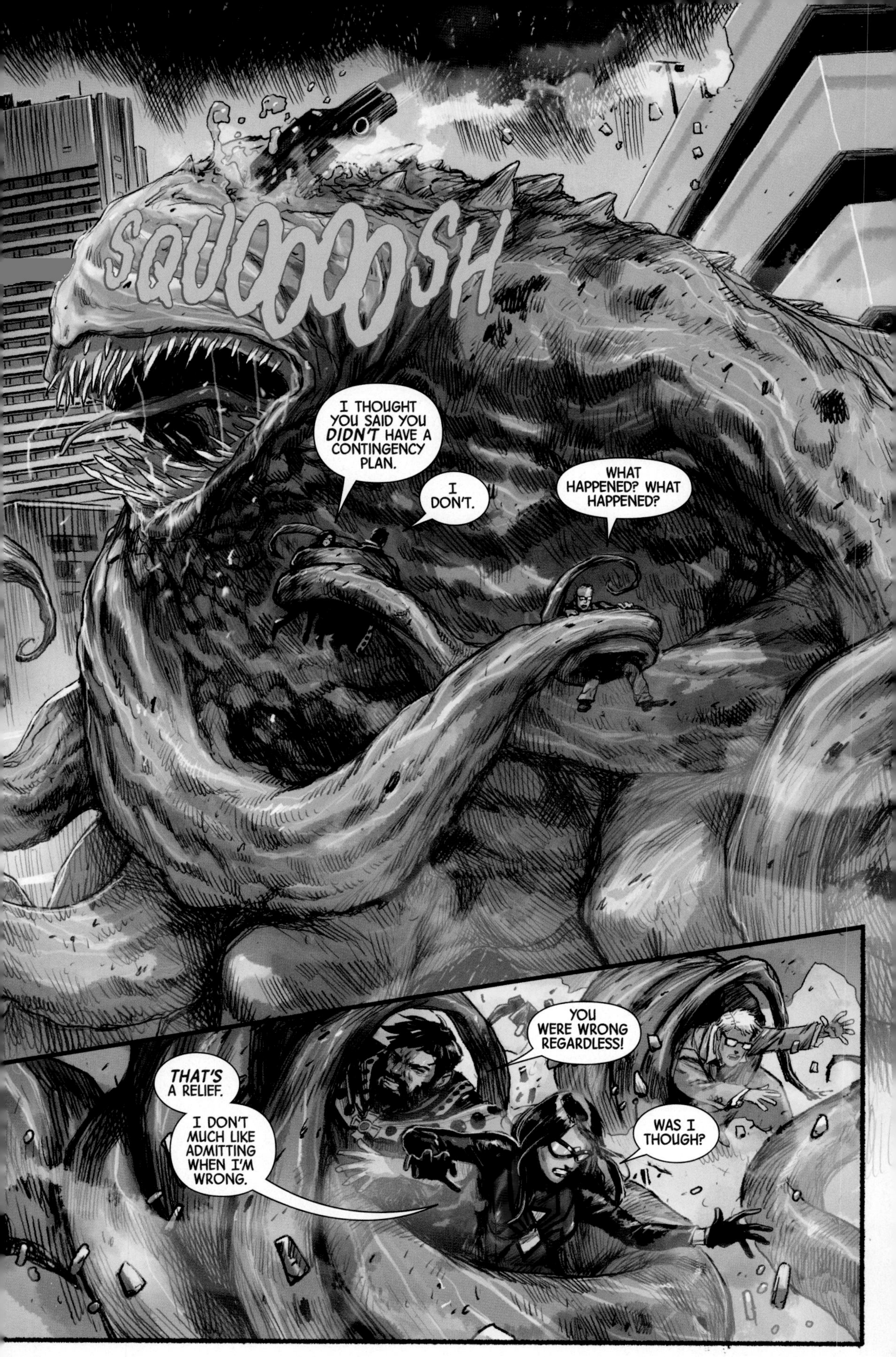
SQUOOOOSH
I THOUGHT YOU SAID YOU DIDN'T HAVE A CONTINGENCY PLAN.
I DON'T.
WHAT HAPPENED? WHAT HAPPENED?
THAT'S A RELIEF.
I DON'T MUCH LIKE ADMITTING WHEN I'M WRONG.
YOU WERE WRONG REGARDLESS!
WAS I THOUGH?

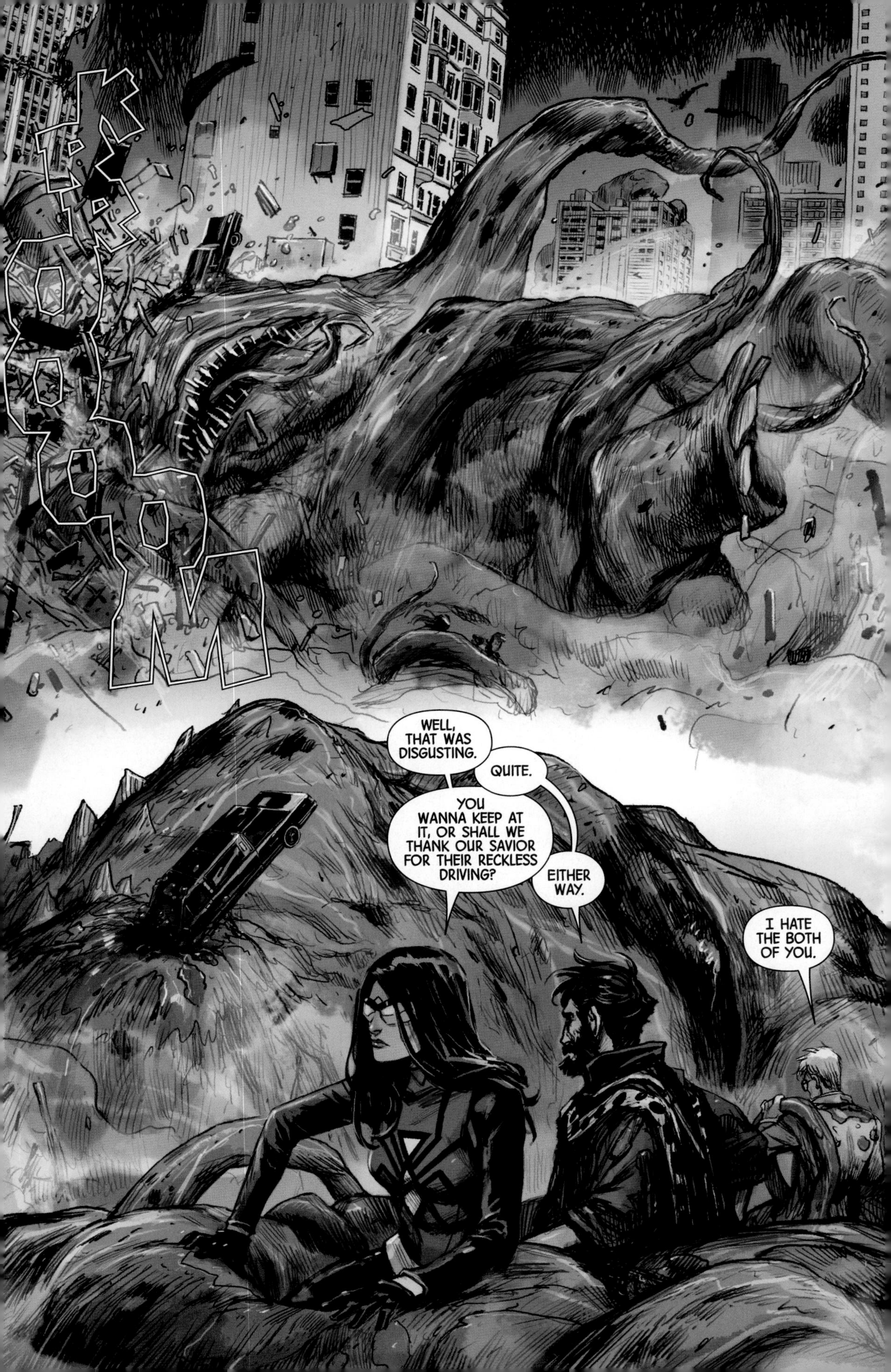
KRAKOOOOM
WELL, THAT WAS DISGUSTING.
QUITE.
YOU WANNA KEEP AT IT, OR SHALL WE THANK OUR SAVIOR FOR THEIR RECKLESS DRIVING?
EITHER WAY.
I HATE THE BOTH OF YOU.

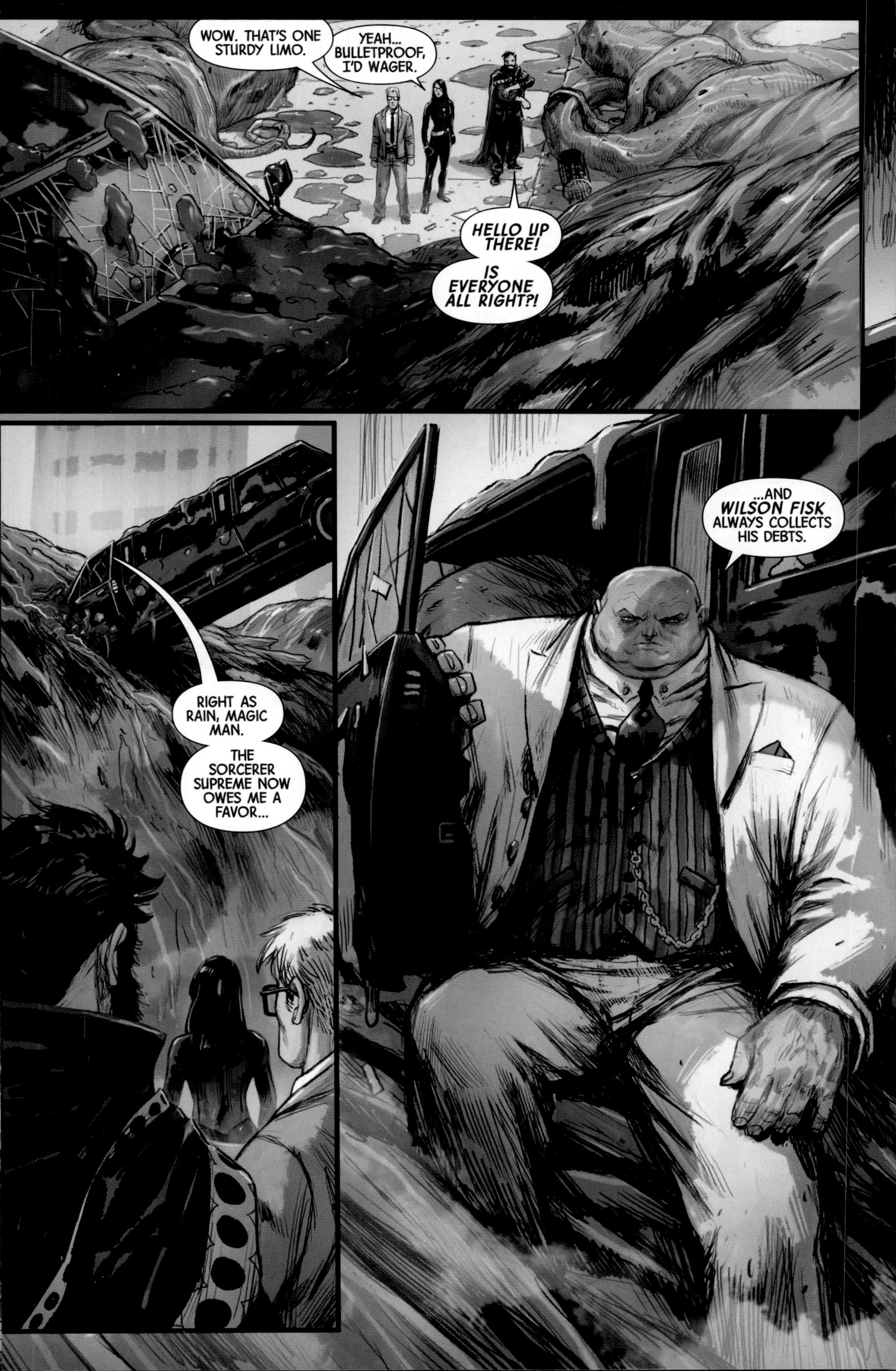
WOW. THAT'S ONE STURDY LIMO.
YEAH... BULLETPROOF, I'D WAGER.
HELLO UP THERE!
IS EVERYONE ALL RIGHT?!
RIGHT AS RAIN, MAGIC MAN.
THE SORCERER SUPREME NOW OWES ME A FAVOR...
...AND WILSON FISK ALWAYS COLLECTS HIS DEBTS.

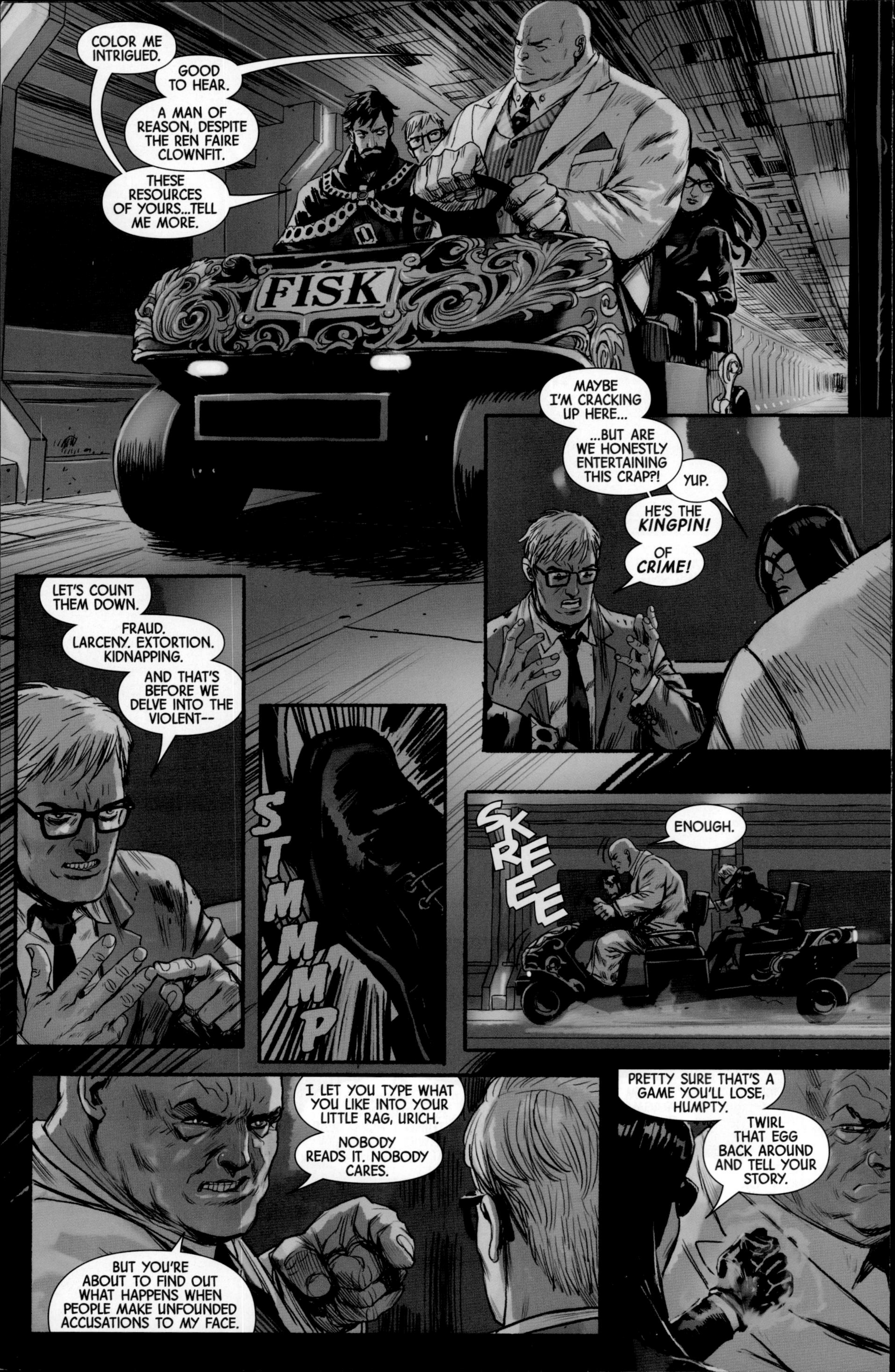

COLOR ME INTRIGUED.
GOOD TO HEAR.
A MAN OF REASON, DESPITE THE REN FAIRE CLOWNFIT.
THESE RESOURCES OF YOURS...TELL ME MORE.
FISK
MAYBE I'M CRACKING UP HERE...
...BUT ARE WE HONESTLY ENTERTAINING THIS CRAP?!
YUP.
HE'S THE KINGPIN!
OF CRIME!
LET'S COUNT THEM DOWN.
FRAUD. LARCENY. EXTORTION. KIDNAPPING.
AND THAT'S BEFORE WE DELVE INTO THE VIOLENT--
STMMMP
SKREEE
ENOUGH.
I LET YOU TYPE WHAT YOU LIKE INTO YOUR LITTLE RAG, URICH.
NOBODY READS IT. NOBODY CARES.
BUT YOU'RE ABOUT TO FIND OUT WHAT HAPPENS WHEN PEOPLE MAKE UNFOUNDED ACCUSATIONS TO MY FACE.
PRETTY SURE THAT'S A GAME YOU'LL LOSE, HUMPTY.
TWIRL THAT EGG BACK AROUND AND TELL YOUR STORY.

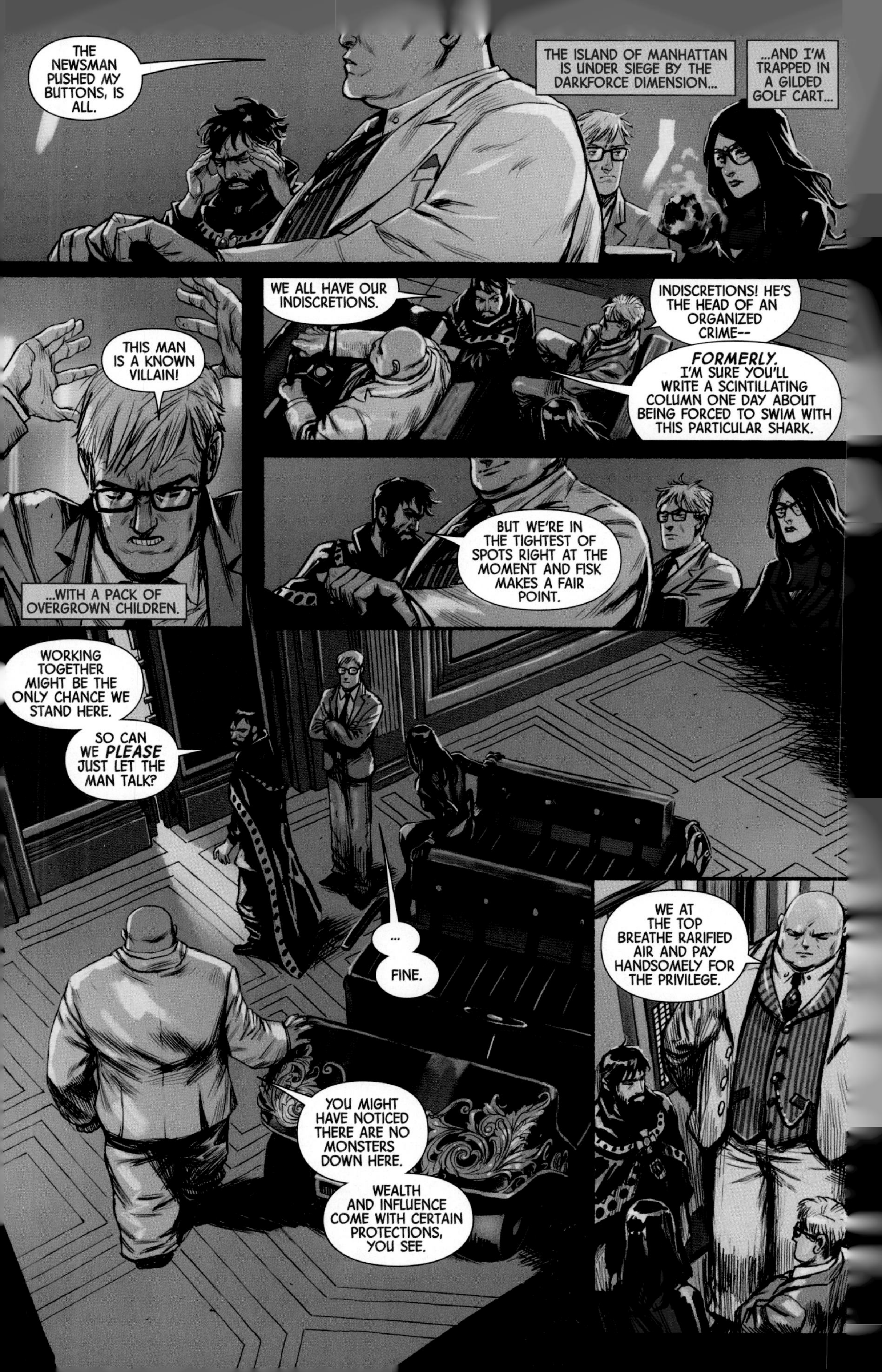
THE NEWSMAN PUSHED MY BUTTONS, IS ALL.
THE ISLAND OF MANHATTAN IS UNDER SIEGE BY THE DARKFORCE DIMENSION...
...AND I'M TRAPPED IN A GILDED GOLF CART...
THIS MAN IS A KNOWN VILLAIN!
...WITH A PACK OF OVERGROWN CHILDREN.
WE ALL HAVE OUR INDISCRETIONS.
INDISCRETIONS! HE'S THE HEAD OF AN ORGANIZED CRIME--
FORMERLY. I'M SURE YOU'LL WRITE A SCINTILLATING COLUMN ONE DAY ABOUT BEING FORCED TO SWIM WITH THIS PARTICULAR SHARK.
BUT WE'RE IN THE TIGHTEST OF SPOTS RIGHT AT THE MOMENT AND FISK MAKES A FAIR POINT.
WORKING TOGETHER MIGHT BE THE ONLY CHANCE WE STAND HERE.
SO CAN WE PLEASE JUST LET THE MAN TALK?
...
FINE.
WE AT THE TOP BREATHE RARIFIED AIR AND PAY HANDSOMELY FOR THE PRIVILEGE.
YOU MIGHT HAVE NOTICED THERE ARE NO MONSTERS DOWN HERE.
WEALTH AND INFLUENCE COME WITH CERTAIN PROTECTIONS, YOU SEE.

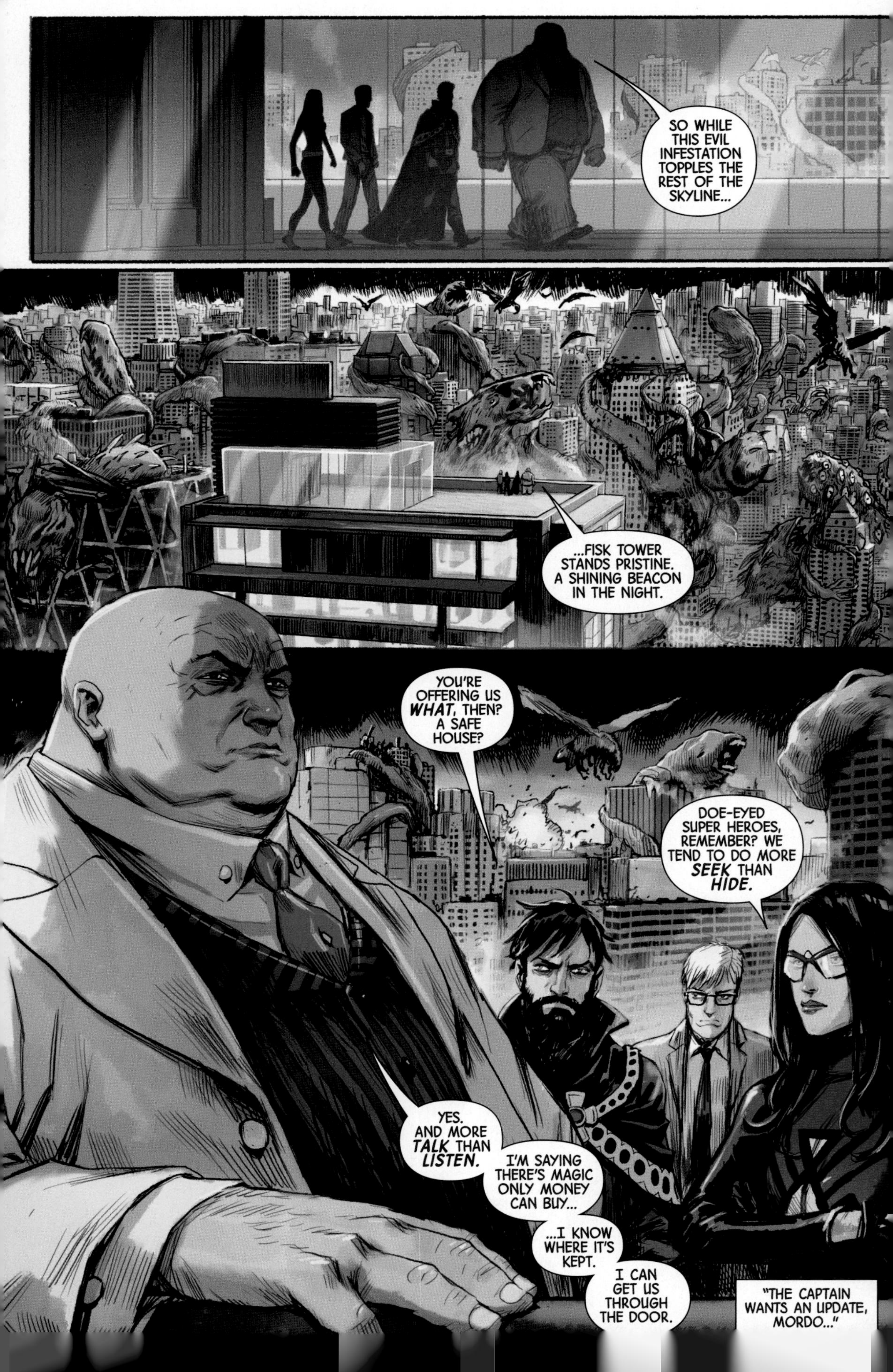
SO WHILE THIS EVIL INFESTATION TOPPLES THE REST OF THE SKYLINE...
...FISK TOWER STANDS PRISTINE. A SHINING BEACON IN THE NIGHT.
YOU'RE OFFERING US WHAT, THEN? A SAFE HOUSE?
DOE-EYED SUPER HEROES, REMEMBER? WE TEND TO DO MORE SEEK THAN HIDE.
YES. AND MORE TALK THAN LISTEN.
I'M SAYING THERE'S MAGIC ONLY MONEY CAN BUY...
...I KNOW WHERE IT'S KEPT.
I CAN GET US THROUGH THE DOOR.
"THE CAPTAIN WANTS AN UPDATE, MORDO..."

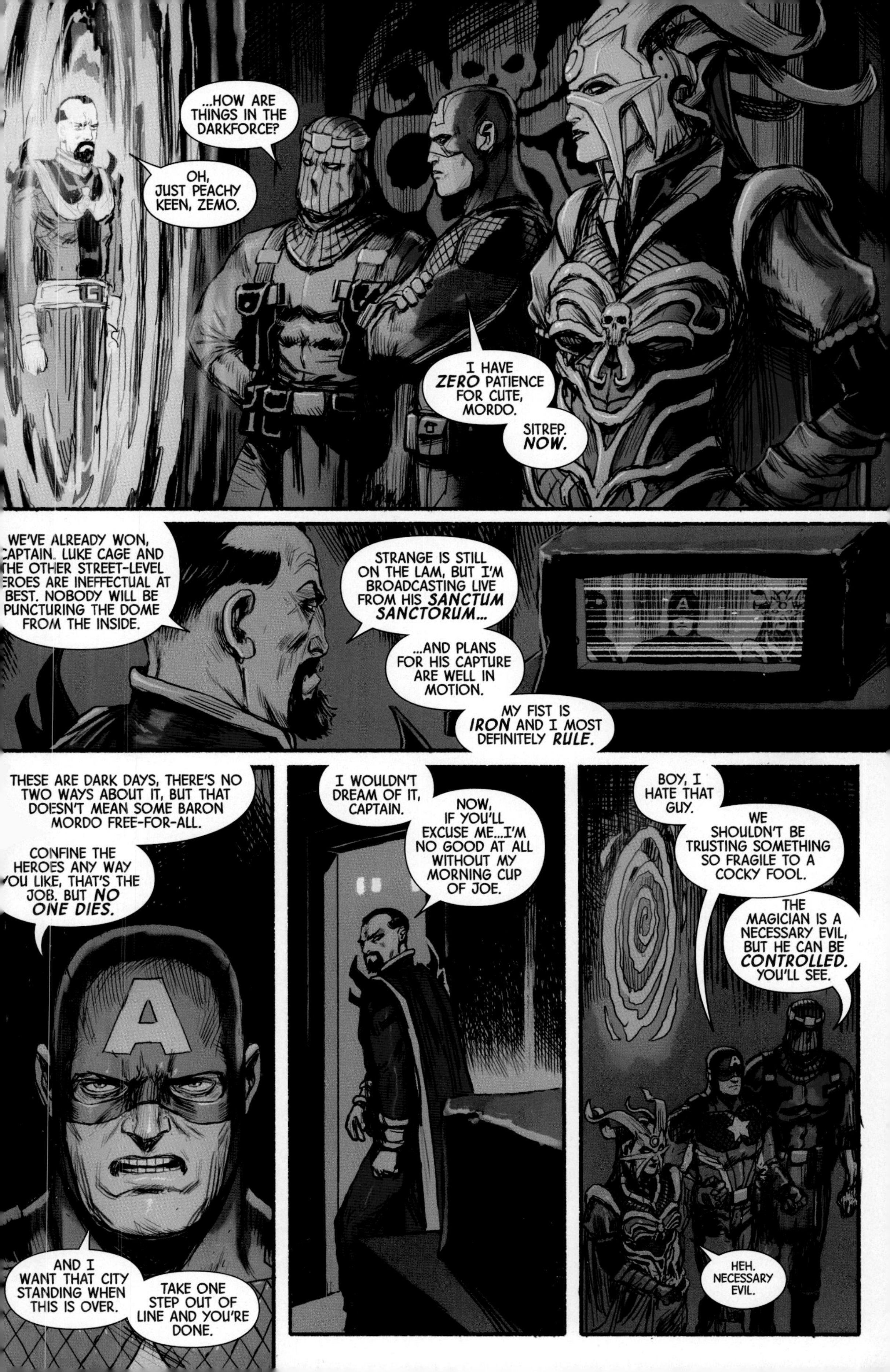
...HOW ARE THINGS IN THE DARKFORCE?
OH, JUST PEACHY KEEN, ZEMO.
I HAVE ZERO PATIENCE FOR CUTE, MORDO.
SITREP. NOW.
WE'VE ALREADY WON, CAPTAIN. LUKE CAGE AND THE OTHER STREET-LEVEL HEROES ARE INEFFECTUAL AT BEST. NOBODY WILL BE PUNCTURING THE DOME FROM THE INSIDE.
STRANGE IS STILL ON THE LAM, BUT I'M BROADCASTING LIVE FROM HIS SANCTUM SANCTORUM...
...AND PLANS FOR HIS CAPTURE ARE WELL IN MOTION.
MY FIST IS IRON AND I MOST DEFINITELY RULE.
THESE ARE DARK DAYS, THERE'S NO TWO WAYS ABOUT IT, BUT THAT DOESN'T MEAN SOME BARON MORDO FREE-FOR-ALL.
CONFINE THE HEROES ANY WAY YOU LIKE, THAT'S THE JOB. BUT NO ONE DIES.
AND I WANT THAT CITY STANDING WHEN THIS IS OVER.
TAKE ONE STEP OUT OF LINE AND YOU'RE DONE.
I WOULDN'T DREAM OF IT, CAPTAIN.
NOW, IF YOU'LL EXCUSE ME...I'M NO GOOD AT ALL WITHOUT MY MORNING CUP OF JOE.
BOY, I HATE THAT GUY.
WE SHOULDN'T BE TRUSTING SOMETHING SO FRAGILE TO A COCKY FOOL.
THE MAGICIAN IS A NECESSARY EVIL, BUT HE CAN BE CONTROLLED. YOU'LL SEE.
HEH. NECESSARY EVIL.

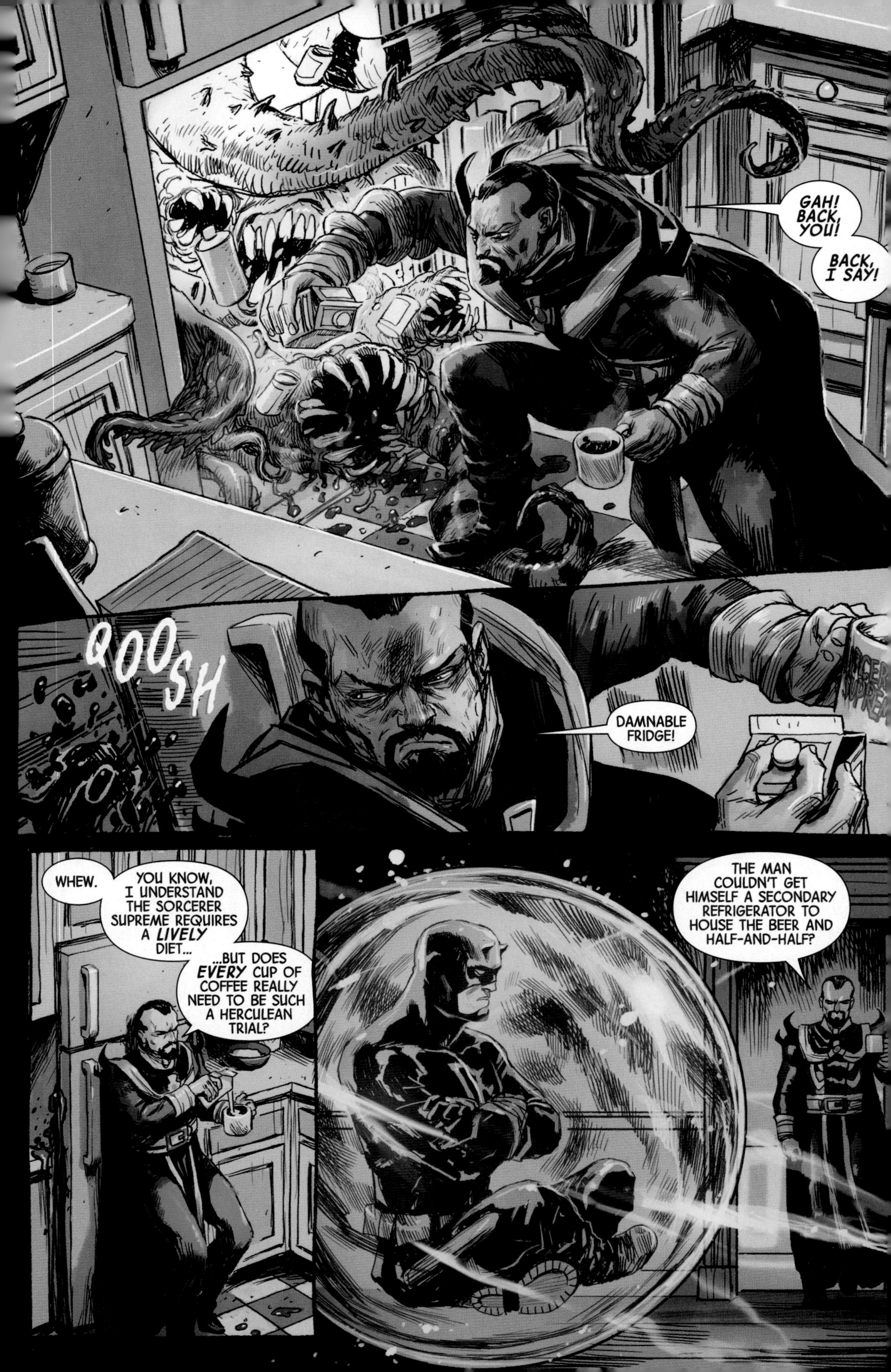
GAH! BACK, YOU!
BACK, I SAY!
QOOSH
DAMNABLE FRIDGE!
WHEW.
YOU KNOW, I UNDERSTAND THE SORCERER SUPREME REQUIRES A *LIVELY* DIET...
...BUT DOES *EVERY* CUP OF COFFEE REALLY NEED TO BE SUCH A HERCULEAN TRIAL?
THE MAN COULDN'T GET HIMSELF A SECONDARY REFRIGERATOR TO HOUSE THE BEER AND HALF-AND-HALF?

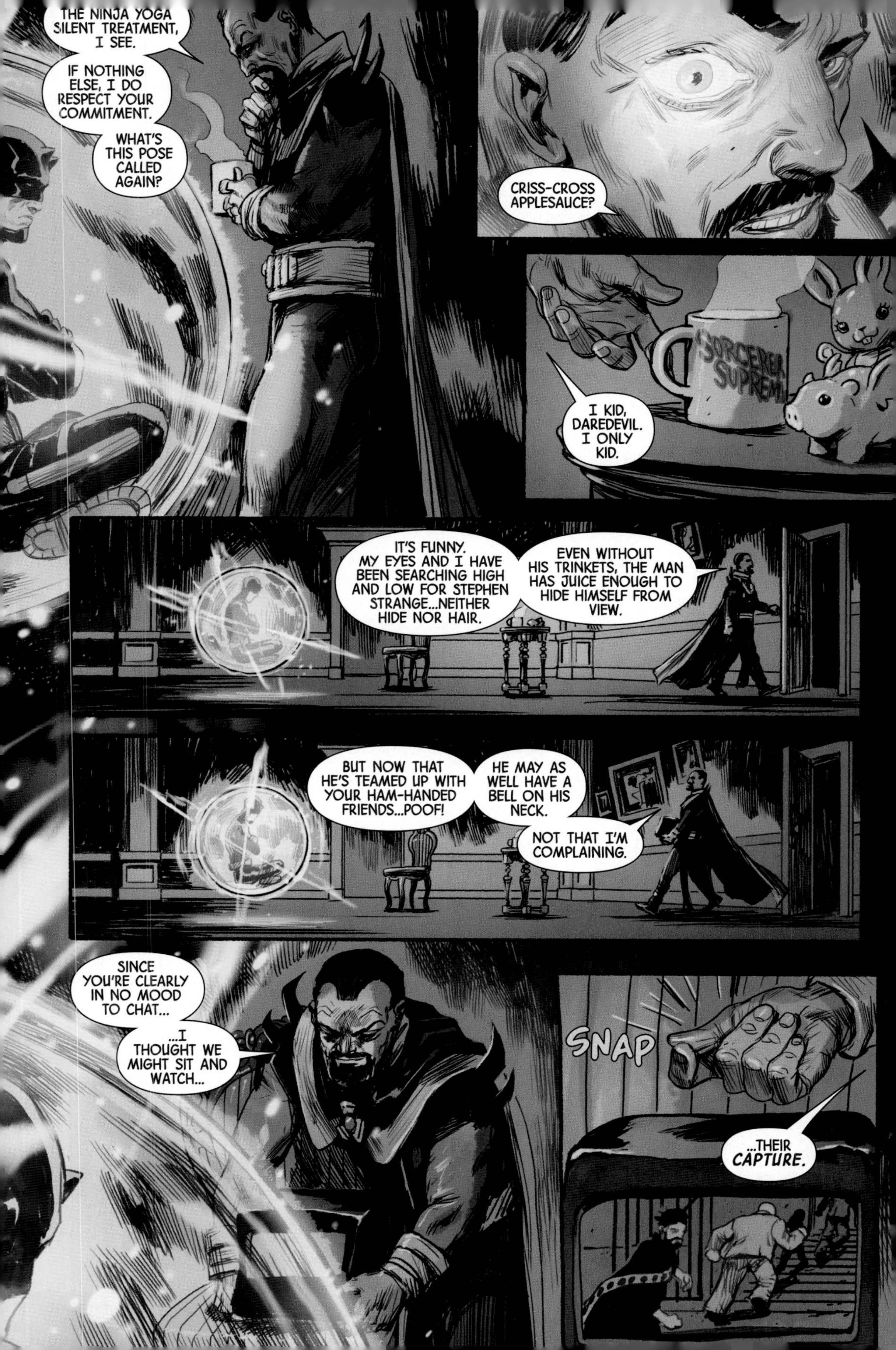
THE NINJA YOGA SILENT TREATMENT, I SEE.
IF NOTHING ELSE, I DO RESPECT YOUR COMMITMENT.
WHAT'S THIS POSE CALLED AGAIN?
CRISS-CROSS APPLESAUCE?
SORCERER SUPREME
I KID, DAREDEVIL. I ONLY KID.
IT'S FUNNY. MY EYES AND I HAVE BEEN SEARCHING HIGH AND LOW FOR STEPHEN STRANGE...NEITHER HIDE NOR HAIR.
EVEN WITHOUT HIS TRINKETS, THE MAN HAS JUICE ENOUGH TO HIDE HIMSELF FROM VIEW.
BUT NOW THAT HE'S TEAMED UP WITH YOUR HAM-HANDED FRIENDS...POOF!
HE MAY AS WELL HAVE A BELL ON HIS NECK.
NOT THAT I'M COMPLAINING.
SINCE YOU'RE CLEARLY IN NO MOOD TO CHAT...
...I THOUGHT WE MIGHT SIT AND WATCH...
SNAP
...THEIR CAPTURE.

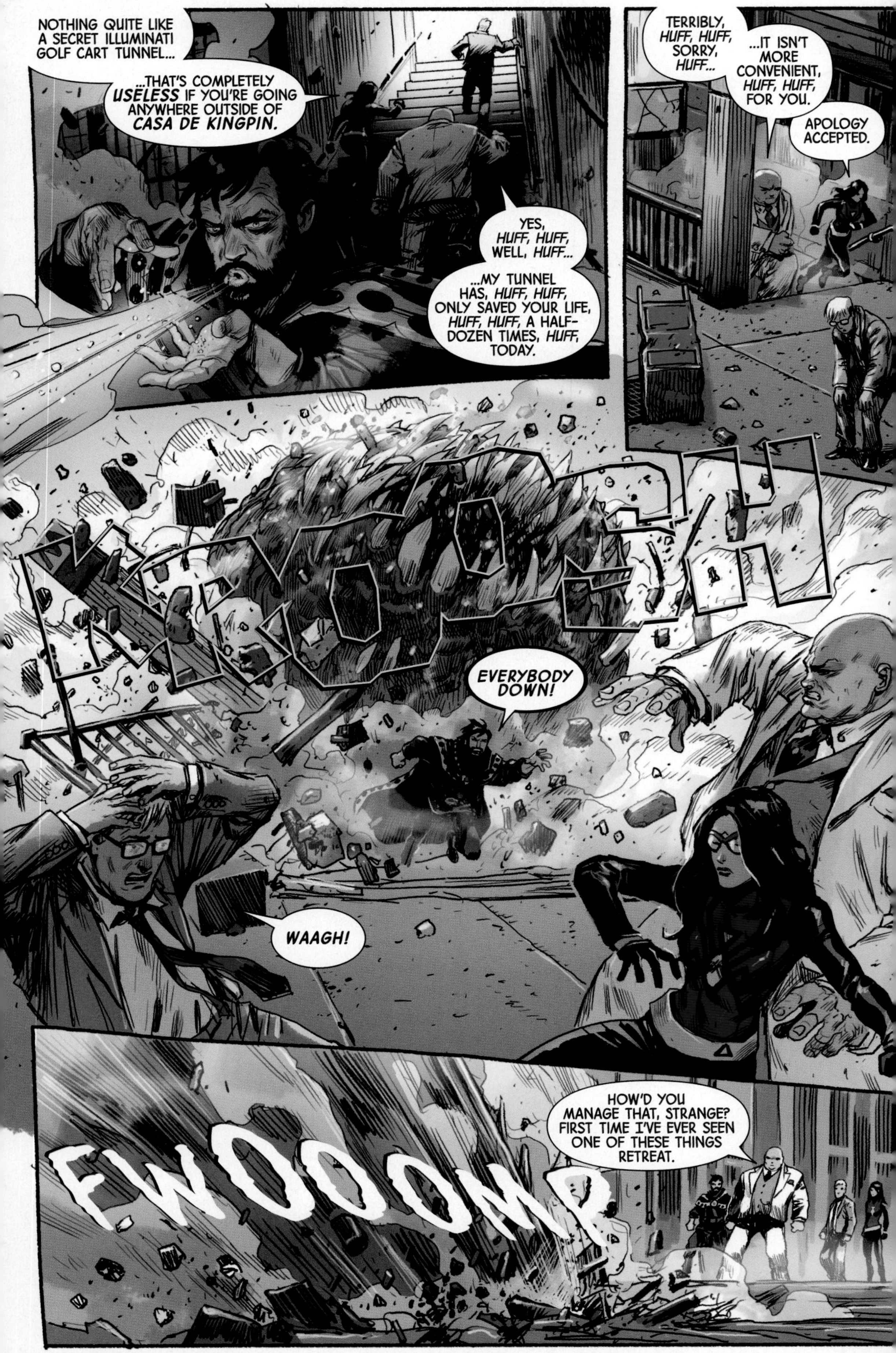
NOTHING QUITE LIKE A SECRET ILLUMINATI GOLF CART TUNNEL...
...THAT'S COMPLETELY USELESS IF YOU'RE GOING ANYWHERE OUTSIDE OF CASA DE KINGPIN.
YES, HUFF, HUFF, WELL, HUFF...
...MY TUNNEL HAS, HUFF, HUFF, ONLY SAVED YOUR LIFE, HUFF, HUFF, A HALF-DOZEN TIMES, HUFF, TODAY.
TERRIBLY, HUFF, HUFF, SORRY, HUFF...
...IT ISN'T MORE CONVENIENT, HUFF, HUFF, FOR YOU.
APOLOGY ACCEPTED.
EVERYBODY DOWN!
WAAGH!
FWOOOMP
HOW'D YOU MANAGE THAT, STRANGE? FIRST TIME I'VE EVER SEEN ONE OF THESE THINGS RETREAT.

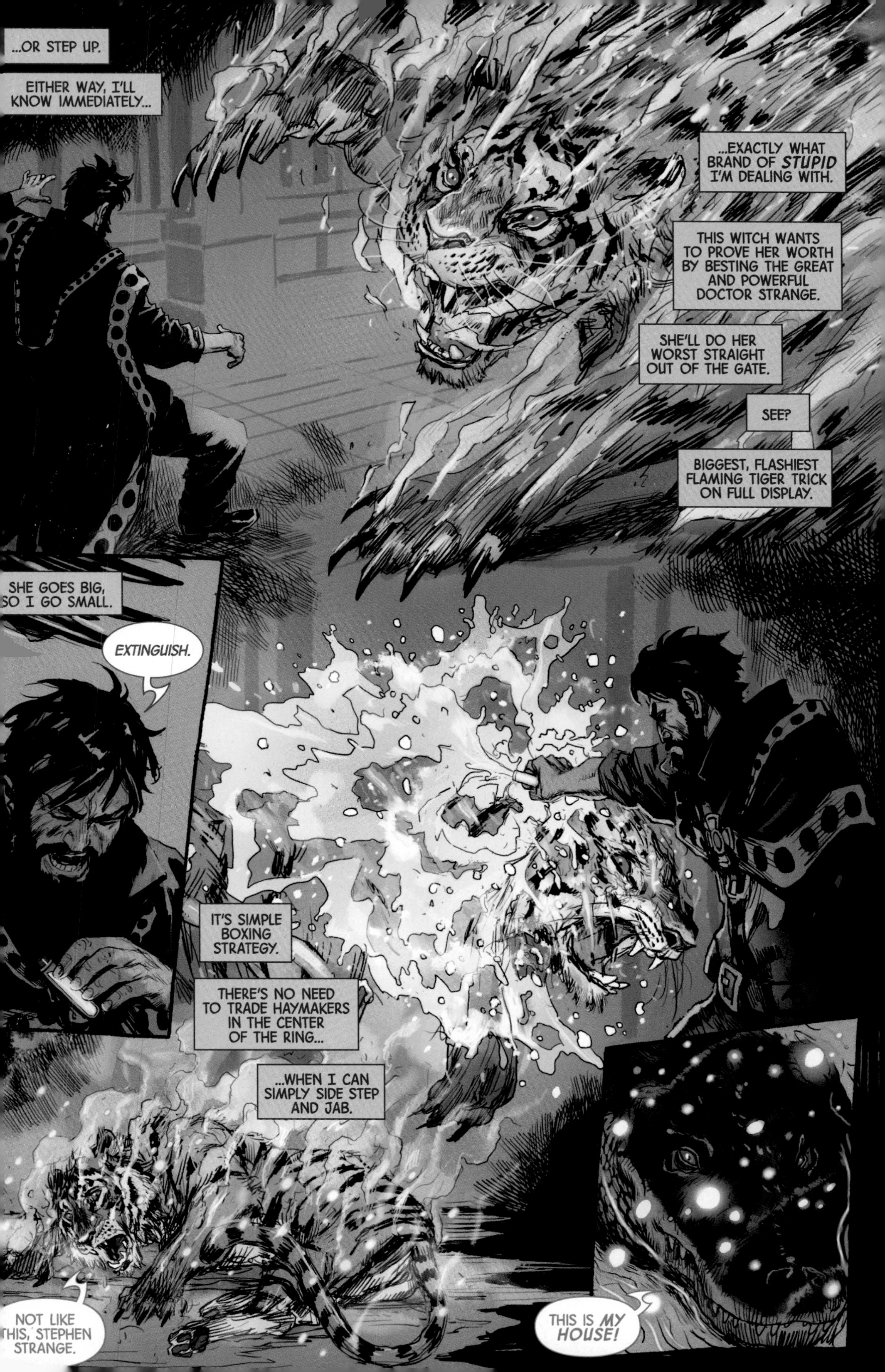
...OR STEP UP.
EITHER WAY, I'LL KNOW IMMEDIATELY...
...EXACTLY WHAT BRAND OF *STUPID* I'M DEALING WITH.
THIS WITCH WANTS TO PROVE HER WORTH BY BESTING THE GREAT AND POWERFUL DOCTOR STRANGE.
SHE'LL DO HER WORST STRAIGHT OUT OF THE GATE.
SEE?
BIGGEST, FLASHIEST FLAMING TIGER TRICK ON FULL DISPLAY.
SHE GOES BIG, SO I GO SMALL.
EXTINGUISH.
IT'S SIMPLE BOXING STRATEGY.
THERE'S NO NEED TO TRADE HAYMAKERS IN THE CENTER OF THE RING...
...WHEN I CAN SIMPLY SIDE STEP AND JAB.
NOT LIKE THIS, STEPHEN STRANGE.
THIS IS *MY HOUSE!*

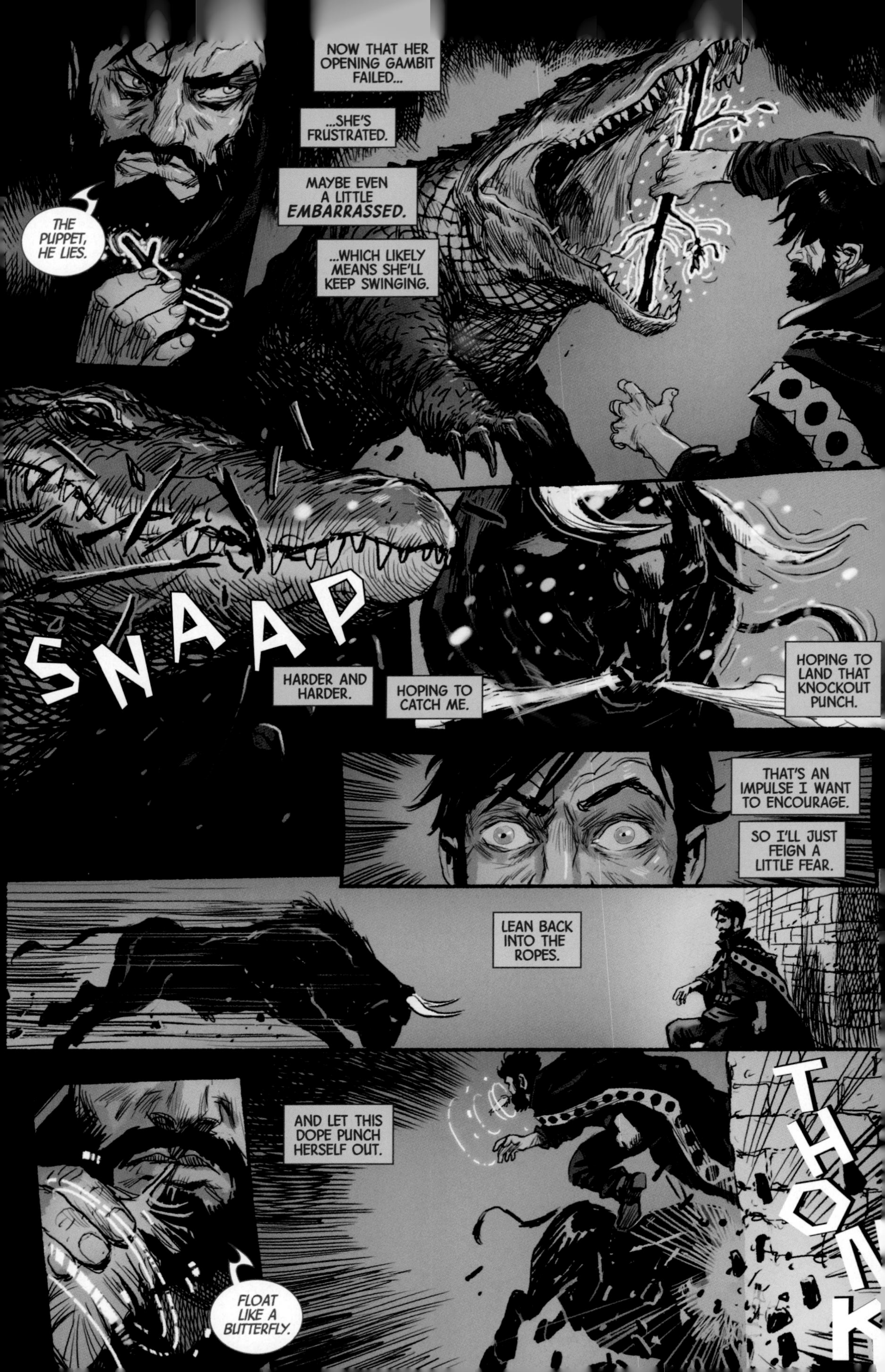
NOW THAT HER OPENING GAMBIT FAILED...
...SHE'S FRUSTRATED.
MAYBE EVEN A LITTLE *EMBARRASSED.*
...WHICH LIKELY MEANS SHE'LL KEEP SWINGING.
THE PUPPET, HE LIES.
SNAAP
HARDER AND HARDER.
HOPING TO CATCH ME.
HOPING TO LAND THAT KNOCKOUT PUNCH.
THAT'S AN IMPULSE I WANT TO ENCOURAGE.
SO I'LL JUST FEIGN A LITTLE FEAR.
LEAN BACK INTO THE ROPES.
AND LET THIS DOPE PUNCH HERSELF OUT.
FLOAT LIKE A BUTTERFLY.
THOOK

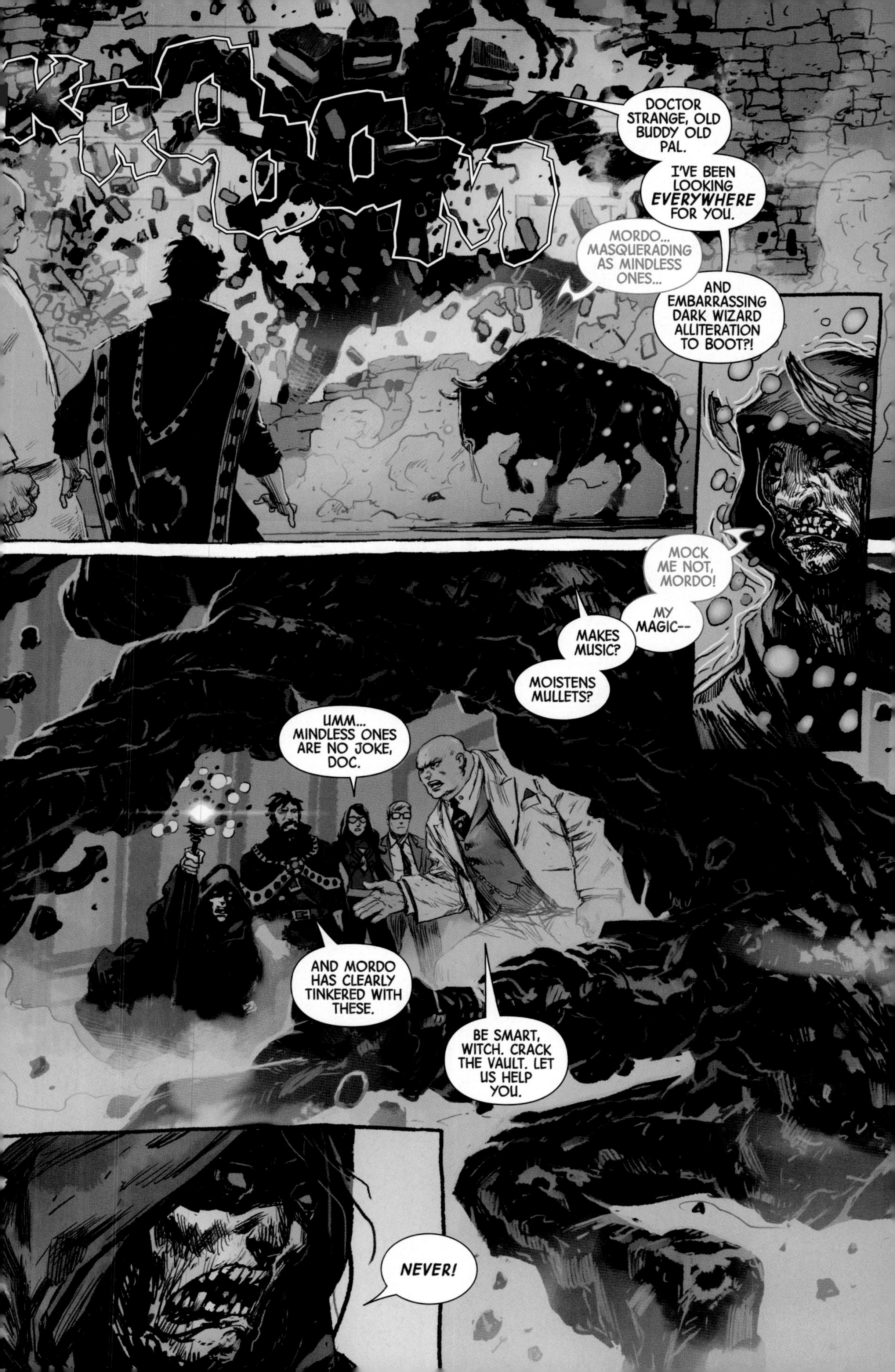
KA-BOOM
DOCTOR STRANGE, OLD BUDDY OLD PAL.
I'VE BEEN LOOKING EVERYWHERE FOR YOU.
MORDO... MASQUERADING AS MINDLESS ONES...
AND EMBARRASSING DARK WIZARD ALLITERATION TO BOOT?!
MOCK ME NOT, MORDO!
MY MAGIC--
MAKES MUSIC?
MOISTENS MULLETS?
UMM... MINDLESS ONES ARE NO JOKE, DOC.
AND MORDO HAS CLEARLY TINKERED WITH THESE.
BE SMART, WITCH. CRACK THE VAULT. LET US HELP YOU.
NEVER!

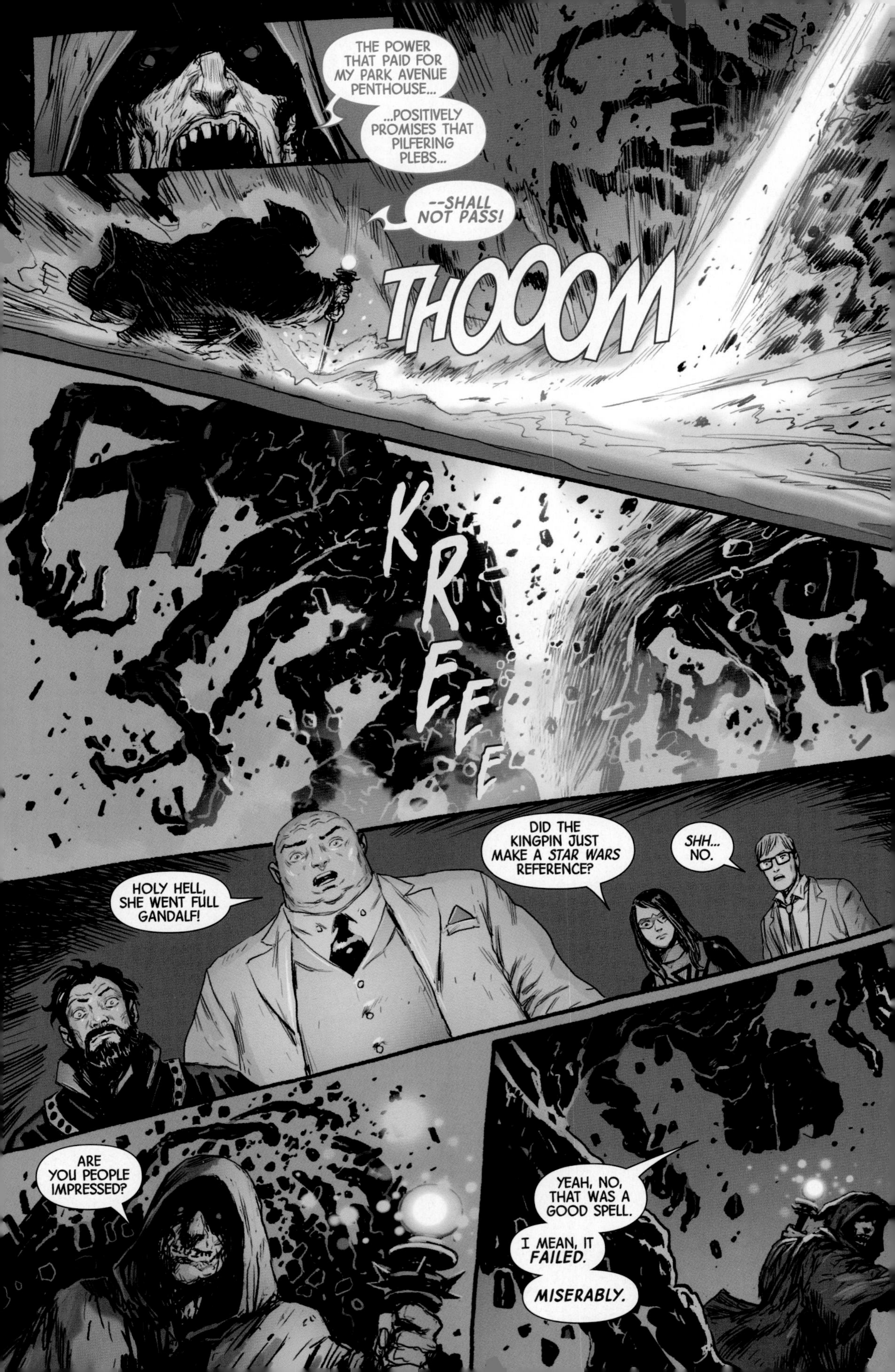
THE POWER THAT PAID FOR MY PARK AVENUE PENTHOUSE...
...POSITIVELY PROMISES THAT PILFERING PLEBS...
--SHALL NOT PASS!
THOOOM
KREEEE
HOLY HELL, SHE WENT FULL GANDALF!
DID THE KINGPIN JUST MAKE A *STAR WARS* REFERENCE?
SHH... NO.
ARE YOU PEOPLE IMPRESSED?
YEAH, NO, THAT WAS A GOOD SPELL.
I MEAN, IT *FAILED.*
MISERABLY.

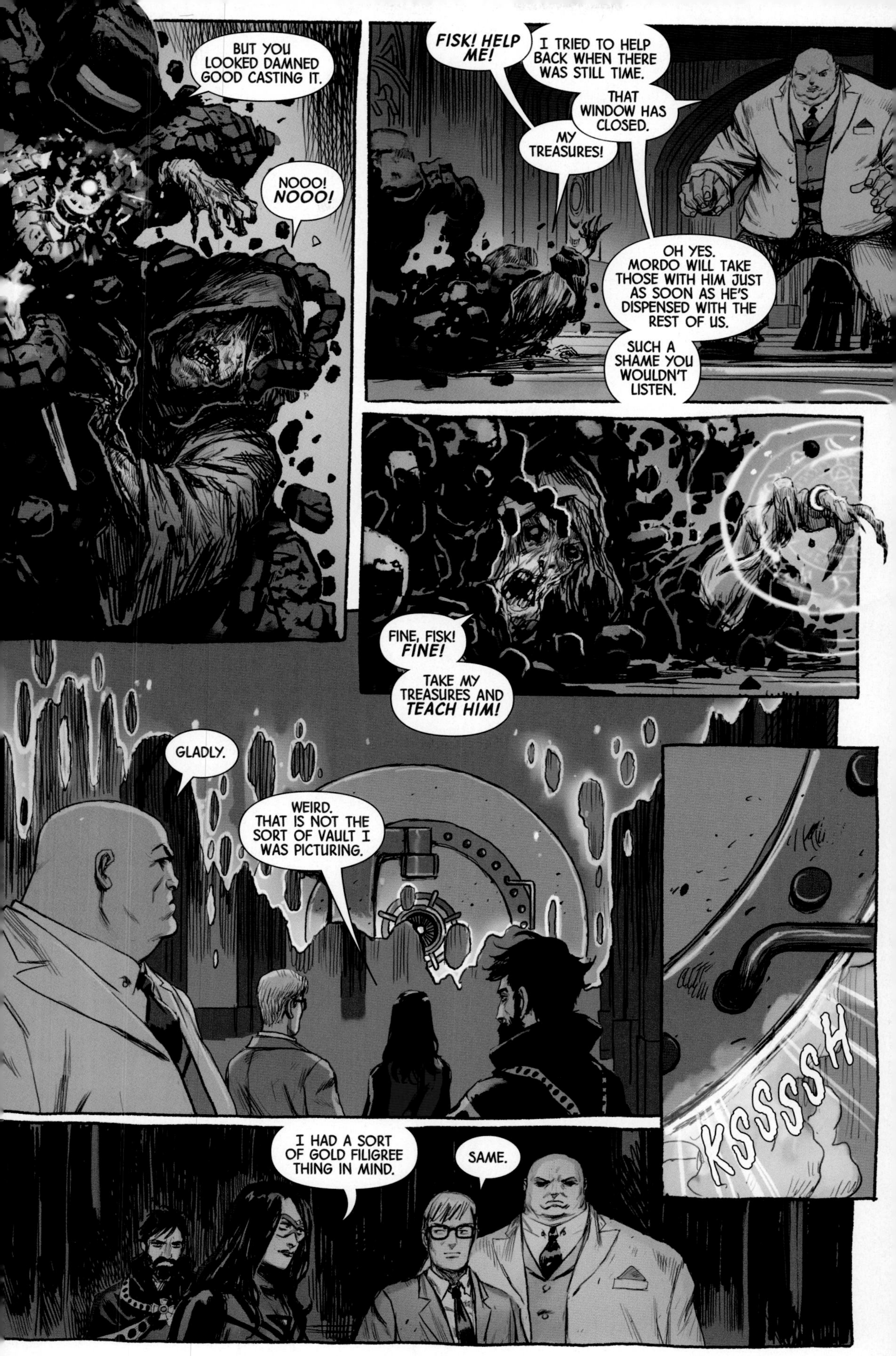

BUT YOU LOOKED DAMNED GOOD CASTING IT.
NOOO! *NOOO!*
FISK! HELP ME!
I TRIED TO HELP BACK WHEN THERE WAS STILL TIME.
THAT WINDOW HAS CLOSED.
MY TREASURES!
OH YES. MORDO WILL TAKE THOSE WITH HIM JUST AS SOON AS HE'S DISPENSED WITH THE REST OF US.
SUCH A SHAME YOU WOULDN'T LISTEN.
FINE, FISK! *FINE!*
TAKE MY TREASURES AND *TEACH HIM!*
GLADLY.
WEIRD. THAT IS NOT THE SORT OF VAULT I WAS PICTURING.
KSSSSSH
I HAD A SORT OF GOLD FILIGREE THING IN MIND.
SAME.

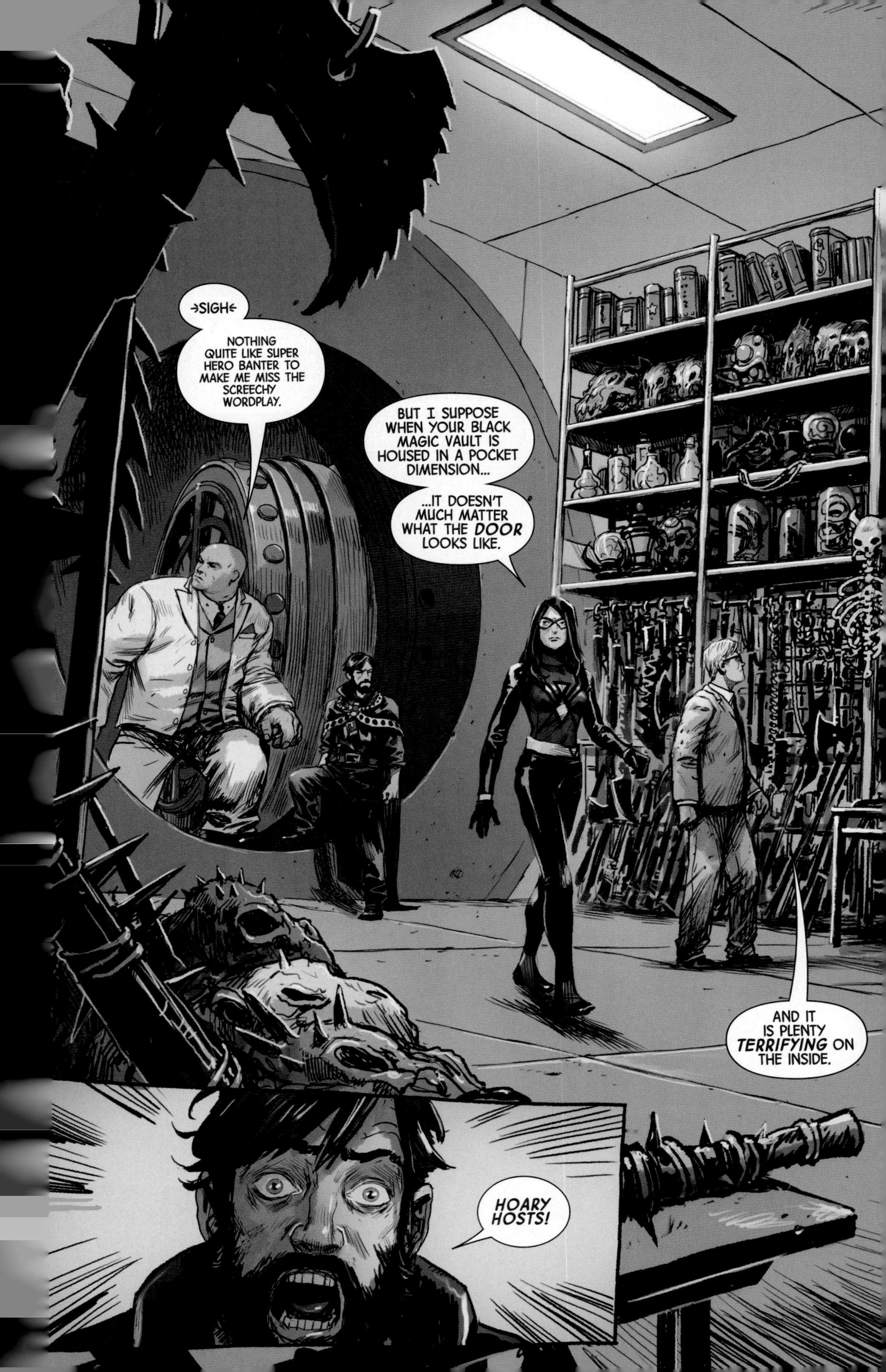

>SIGH<
NOTHING QUITE LIKE SUPER HERO BANTER TO MAKE ME MISS THE SCREECHY WORDPLAY.
BUT I SUPPOSE WHEN YOUR BLACK MAGIC VAULT IS HOUSED IN A POCKET DIMENSION...
...IT DOESN'T MUCH MATTER WHAT THE DOOR LOOKS LIKE.
AND IT IS PLENTY TERRIFYING ON THE INSIDE.
HOARY HOSTS!

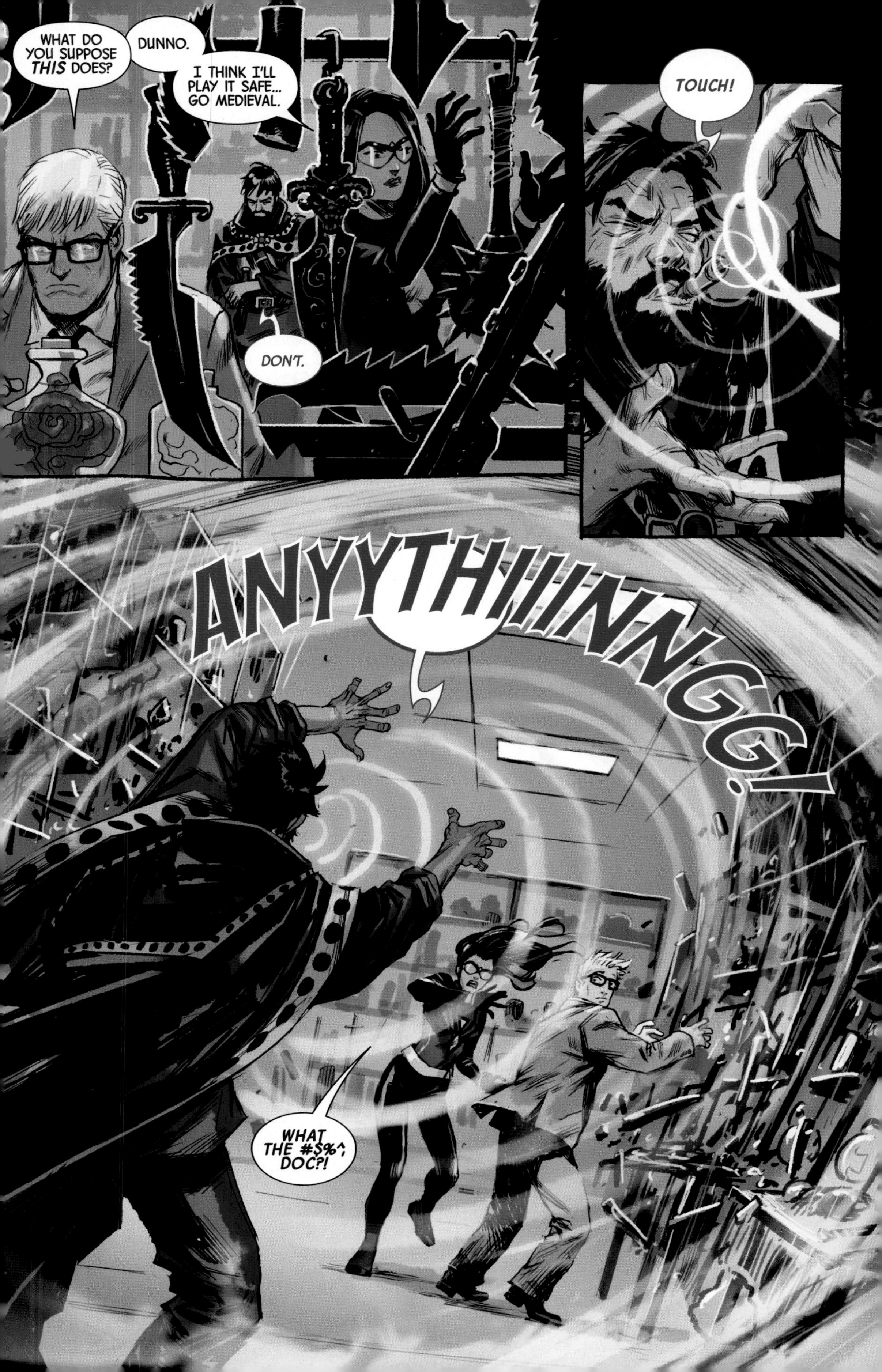
WHAT DO YOU SUPPOSE THIS DOES?
DUNNO.
I THINK I'LL PLAY IT SAFE... GO MEDIEVAL.
DON'T.
TOUCH!
ANYYTHIIINNGG!
WHAT THE #$%^, DOC?!

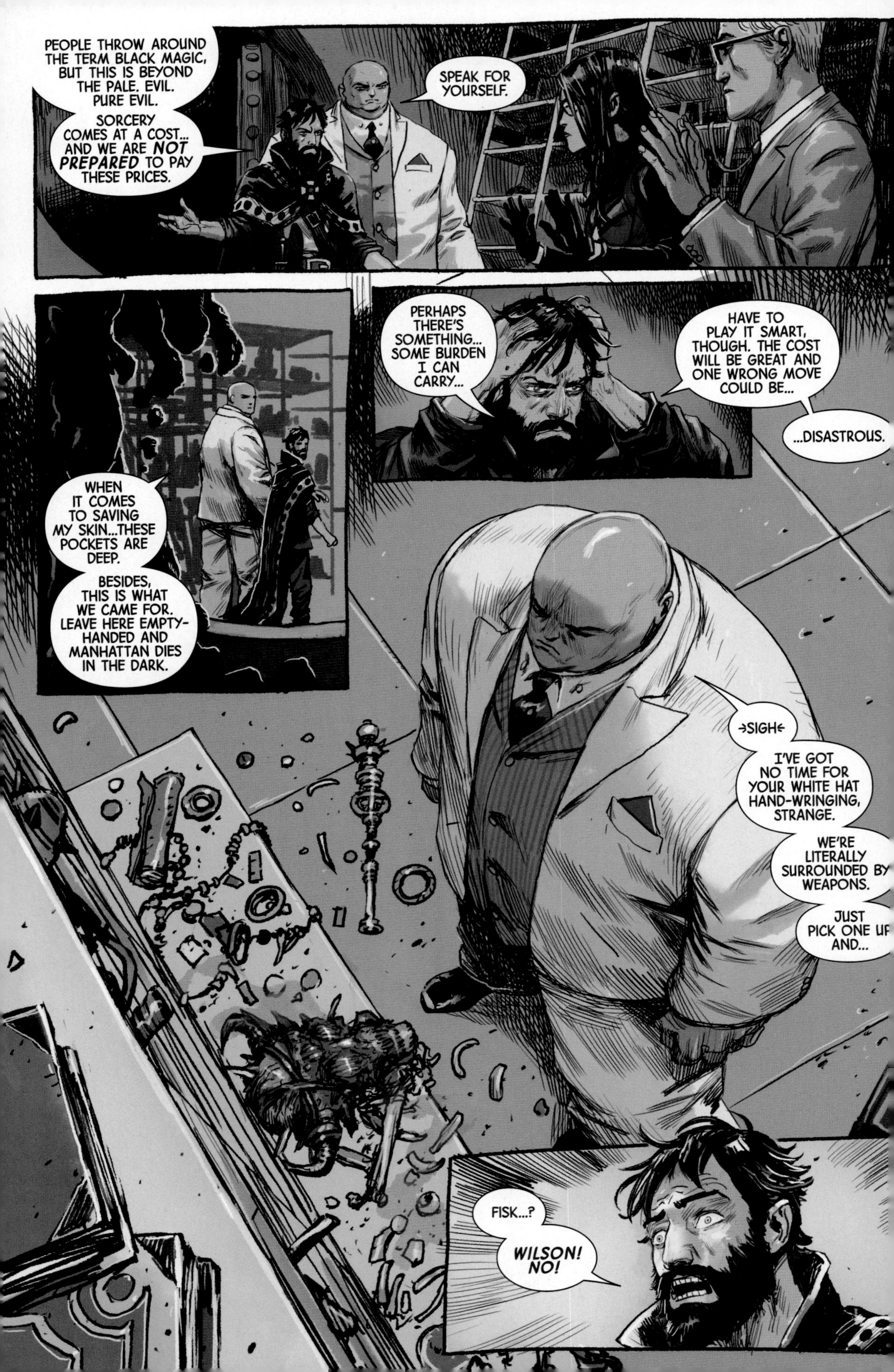

PEOPLE THROW AROUND THE TERM BLACK MAGIC, BUT THIS IS BEYOND THE PALE. EVIL. PURE EVIL.
SORCERY COMES AT A COST... AND WE ARE ***NOT PREPARED*** TO PAY THESE PRICES.
SPEAK FOR YOURSELF.
WHEN IT COMES TO SAVING MY SKIN...THESE POCKETS ARE DEEP.
BESIDES, THIS IS WHAT WE CAME FOR. LEAVE HERE EMPTY-HANDED AND MANHATTAN DIES IN THE DARK.
PERHAPS THERE'S SOMETHING... SOME BURDEN I CAN CARRY...
HAVE TO PLAY IT SMART, THOUGH. THE COST WILL BE GREAT AND ONE WRONG MOVE COULD BE...
...DISASTROUS.
›SIGH‹
I'VE GOT NO TIME FOR YOUR WHITE HAT HAND-WRINGING, STRANGE.
WE'RE LITERALLY SURROUNDED BY WEAPONS.
JUST PICK ONE UP AND...
FISK...?
WILSON! NO!

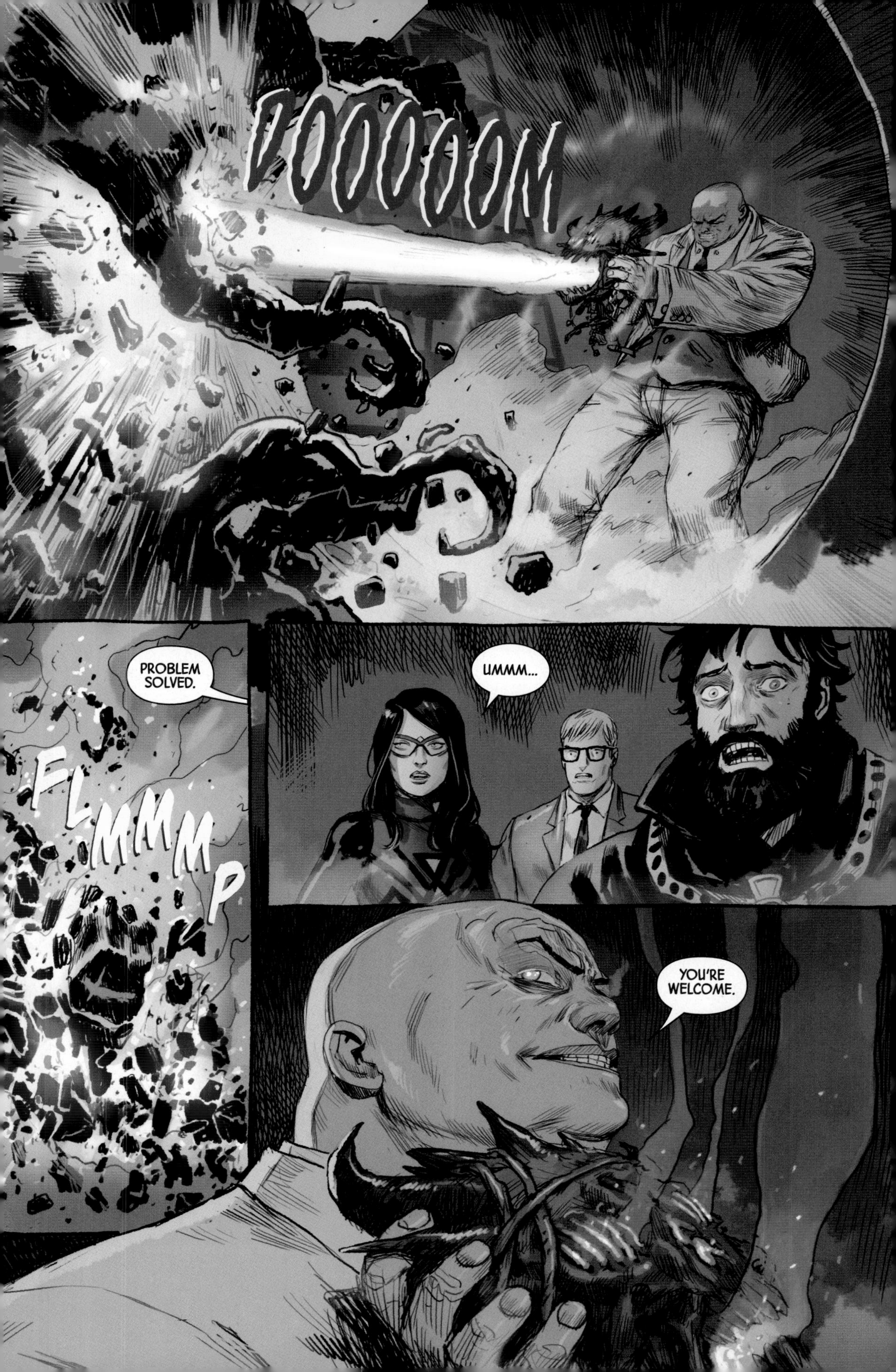
DOOOOOM
PROBLEM SOLVED.
FLMMMMP
UMMM...
YOU'RE WELCOME.

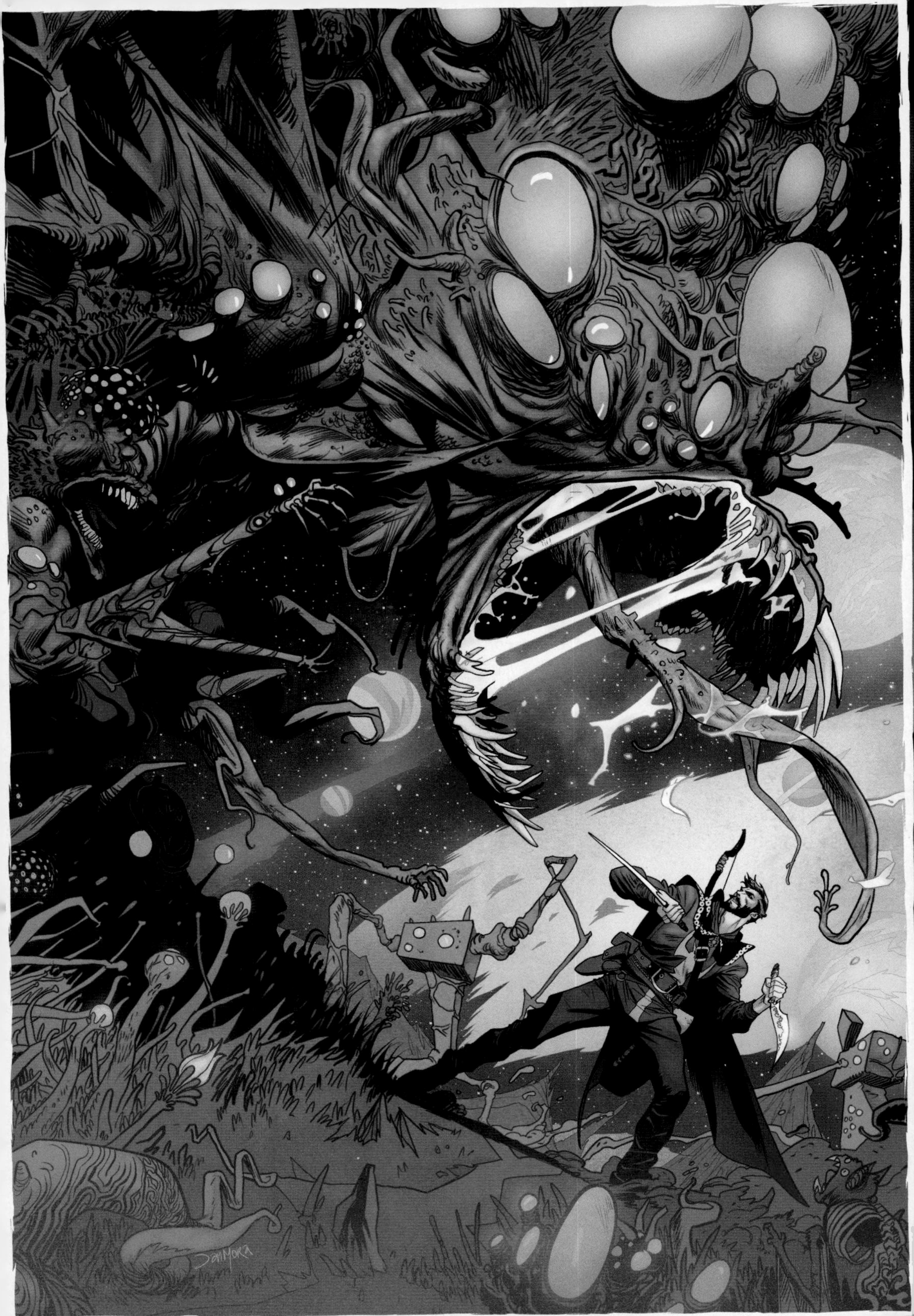
DanMora

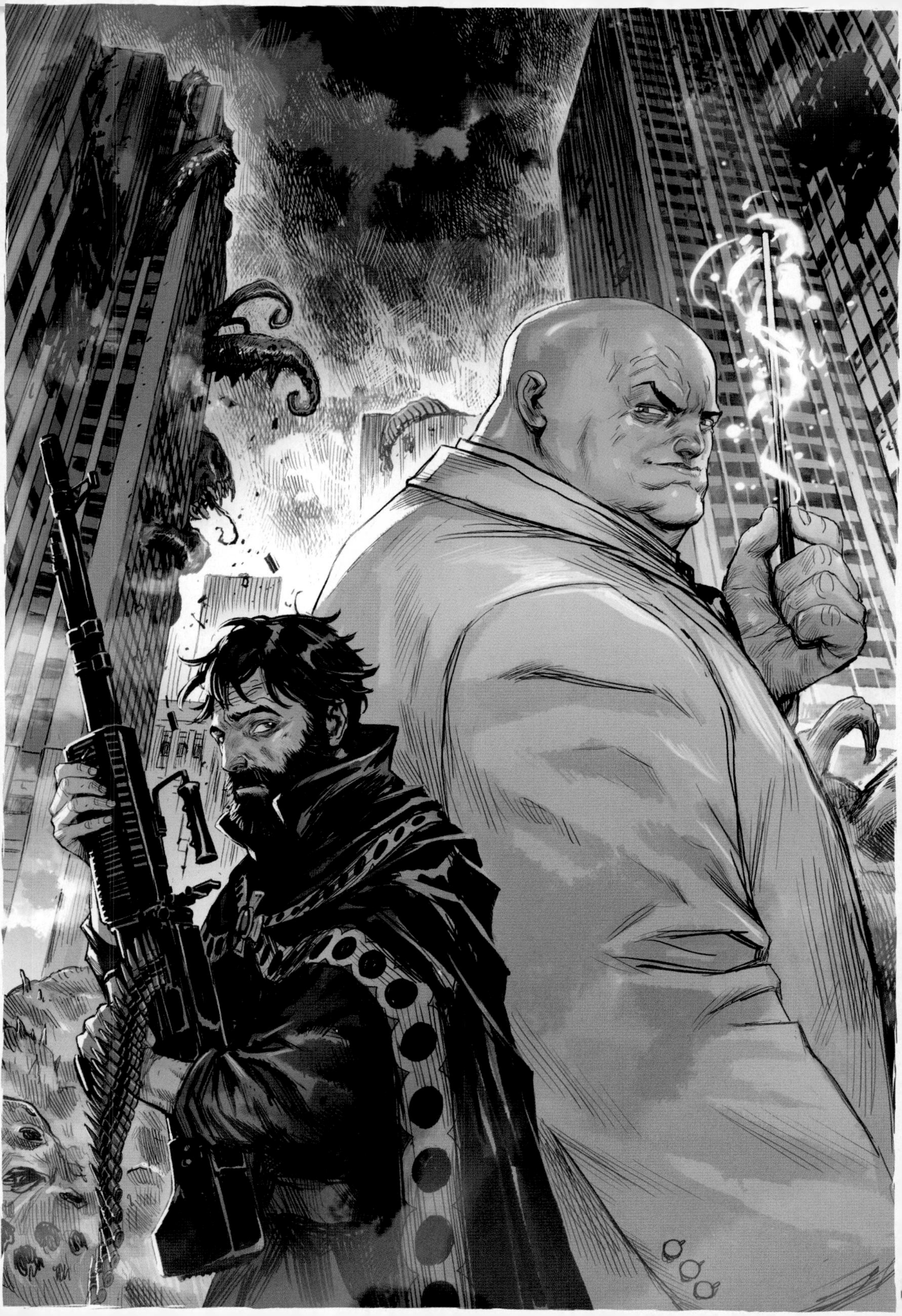

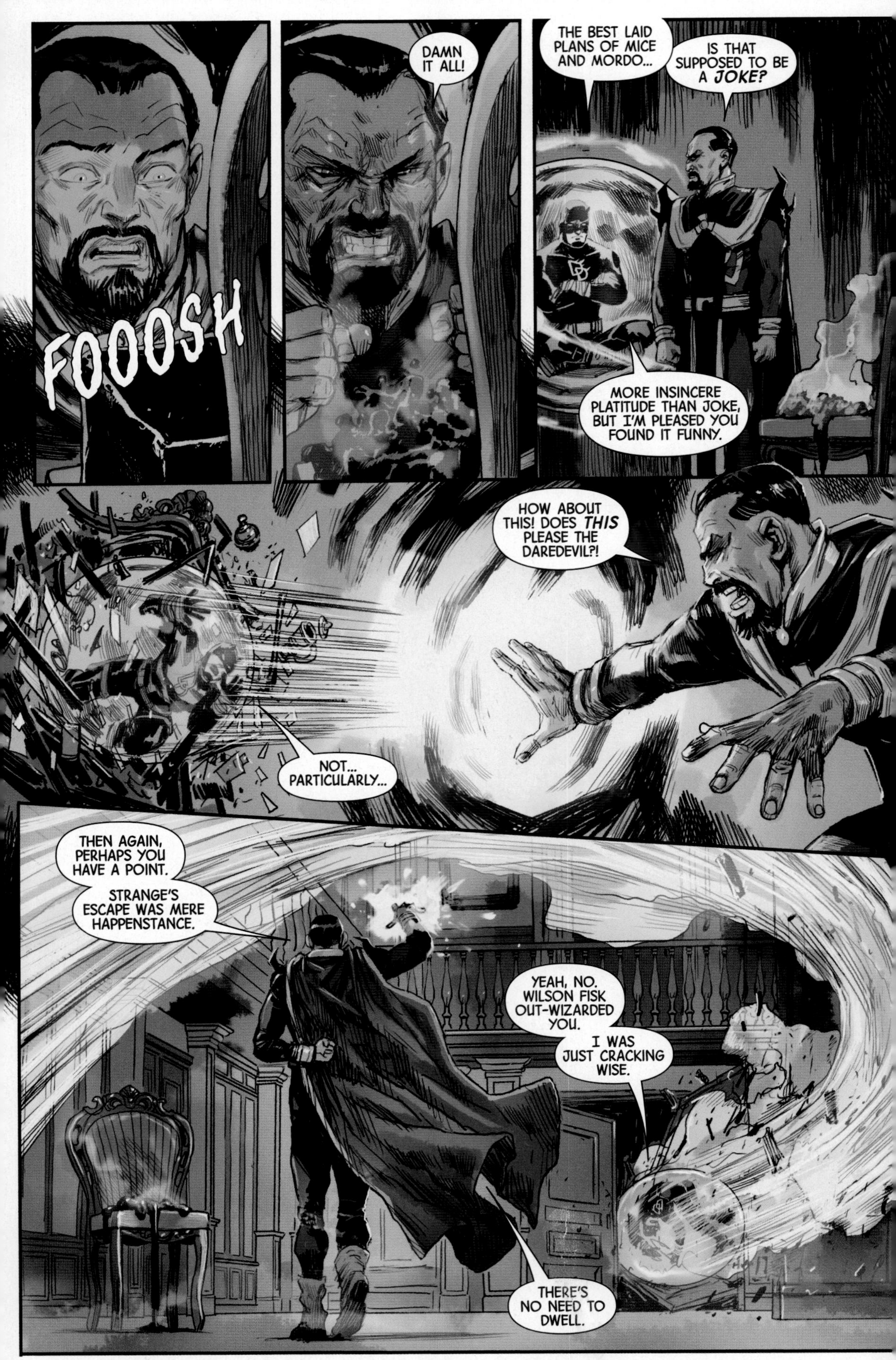
FOOOSH
DAMN IT ALL!
THE BEST LAID PLANS OF MICE AND MORDO...
IS THAT SUPPOSED TO BE A JOKE?
MORE INSINCERE PLATITUDE THAN JOKE, BUT I'M PLEASED YOU FOUND IT FUNNY.
HOW ABOUT THIS! DOES THIS PLEASE THE DAREDEVIL?!
NOT... PARTICULARLY...
THEN AGAIN, PERHAPS YOU HAVE A POINT.
STRANGE'S ESCAPE WAS MERE HAPPENSTANCE.
YEAH, NO. WILSON FISK OUT-WIZARDED YOU.
I WAS JUST CRACKING WISE.
THERE'S NO NEED TO DWELL.

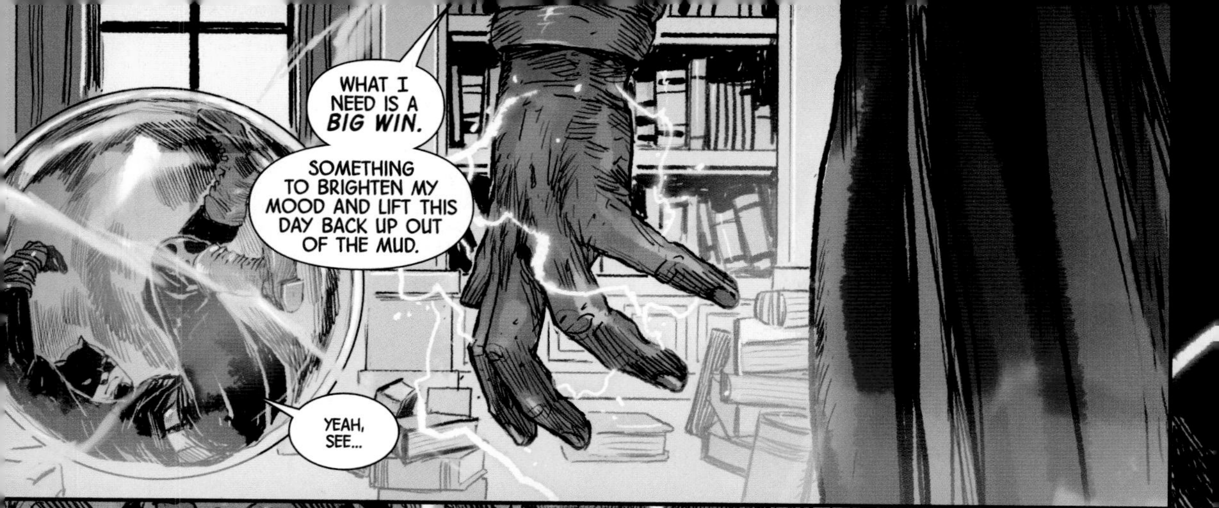
WHAT I NEED IS A *BIG WIN.*
SOMETHING TO BRIGHTEN MY MOOD AND LIFT THIS DAY BACK UP OUT OF THE MUD.
YEAH, SEE...

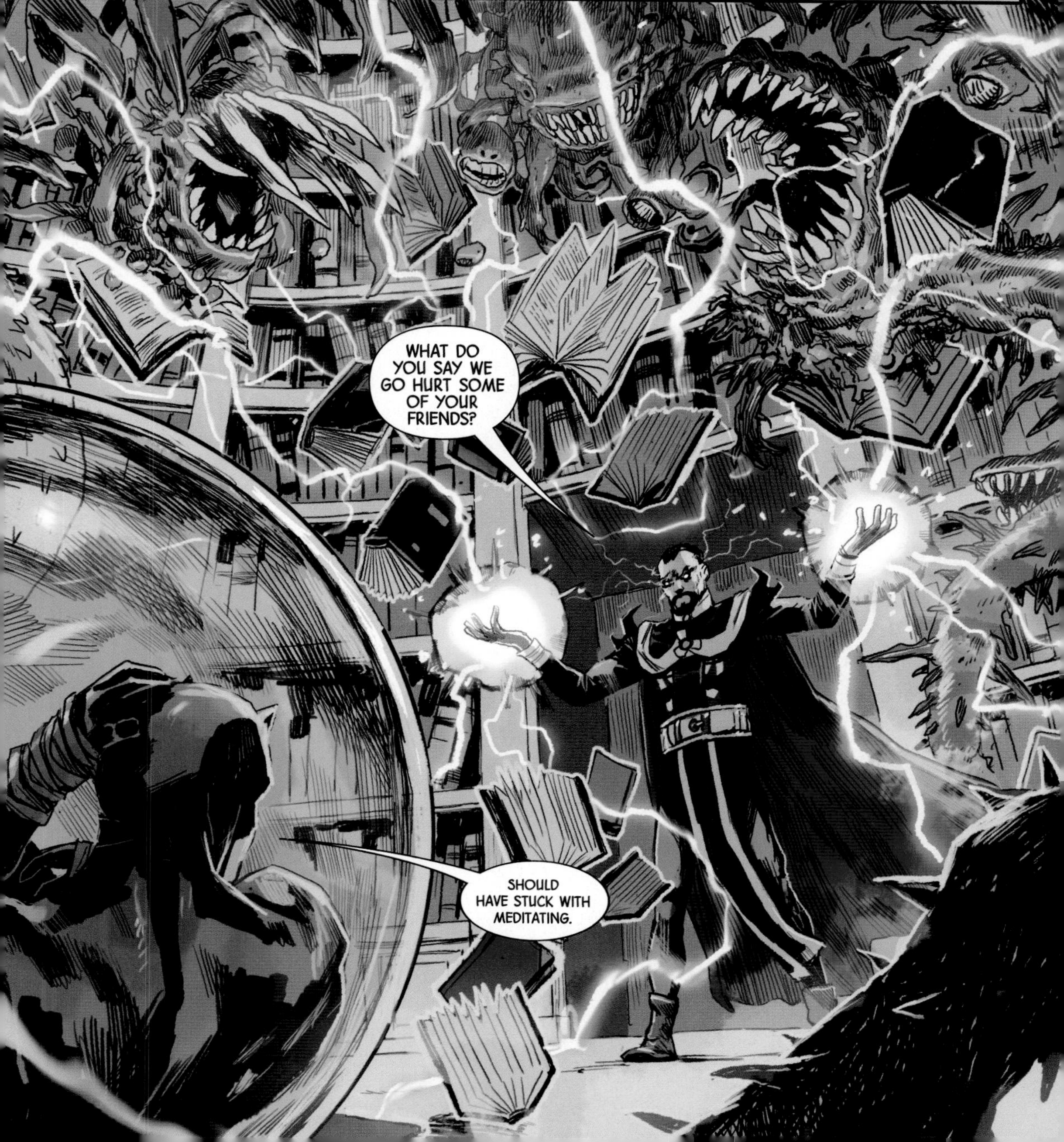
WHAT DO YOU SAY WE GO HURT SOME OF YOUR FRIENDS?
SHOULD HAVE STUCK WITH MEDITATING.

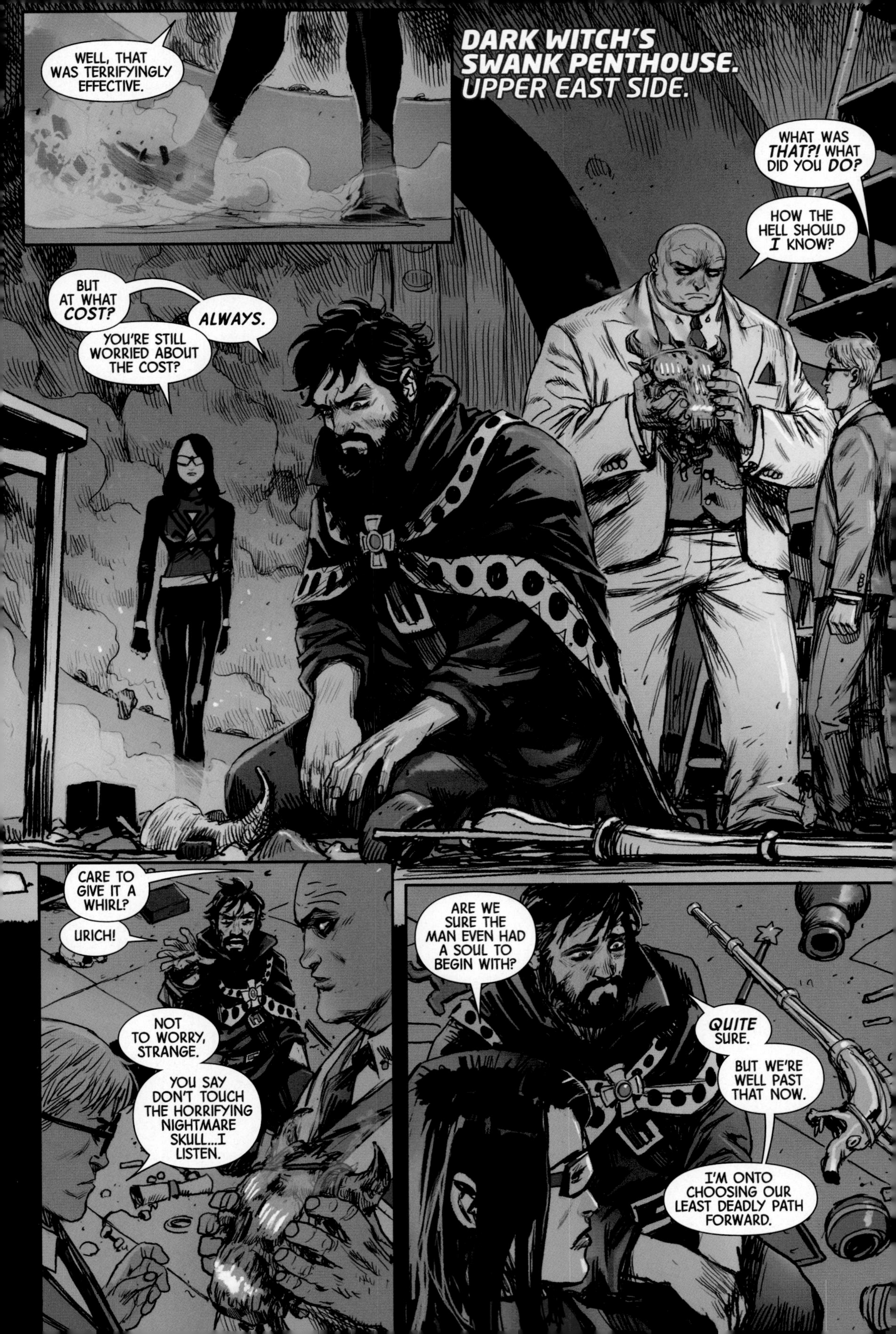
WELL, THAT WAS TERRIFYINGLY EFFECTIVE.
DARK WITCH'S SWANK PENTHOUSE. UPPER EAST SIDE.
WHAT WAS THAT?! WHAT DID YOU DO?
HOW THE HELL SHOULD I KNOW?
BUT AT WHAT COST?
ALWAYS.
YOU'RE STILL WORRIED ABOUT THE COST?
CARE TO GIVE IT A WHIRL?
URICH!
NOT TO WORRY, STRANGE.
YOU SAY DON'T TOUCH THE HORRIFYING NIGHTMARE SKULL...I LISTEN.
ARE WE SURE THE MAN EVEN HAD A SOUL TO BEGIN WITH?
QUITE SURE.
BUT WE'RE WELL PAST THAT NOW.
I'M ONTO CHOOSING OUR LEAST DEADLY PATH FORWARD.

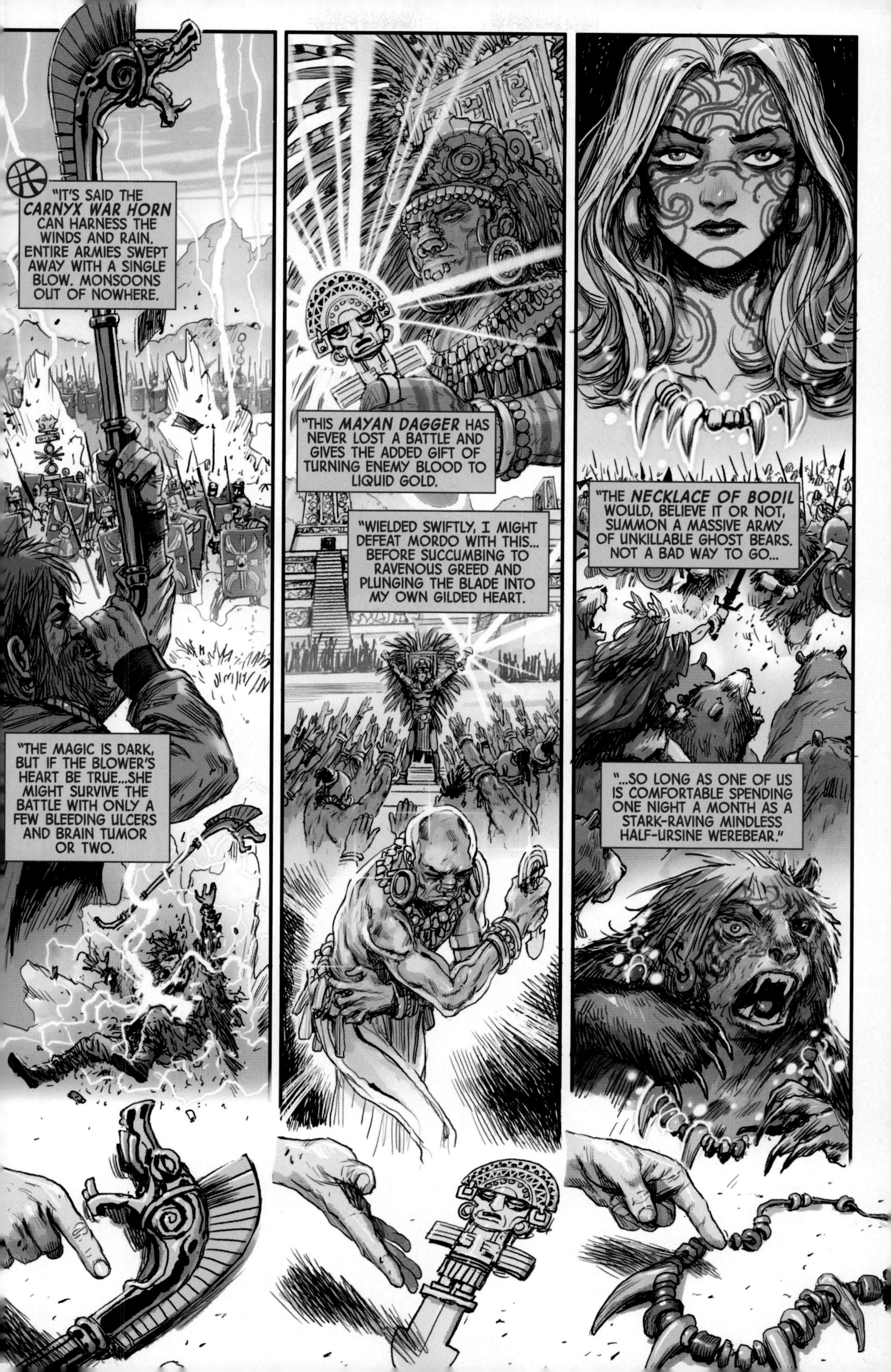
"IT'S SAID THE CARNYX WAR HORN CAN HARNESS THE WINDS AND RAIN. ENTIRE ARMIES SWEPT AWAY WITH A SINGLE BLOW. MONSOONS OUT OF NOWHERE.
"THE MAGIC IS DARK, BUT IF THE BLOWER'S HEART BE TRUE...SHE MIGHT SURVIVE THE BATTLE WITH ONLY A FEW BLEEDING ULCERS AND BRAIN TUMOR OR TWO.
"THIS MAYAN DAGGER HAS NEVER LOST A BATTLE AND GIVES THE ADDED GIFT OF TURNING ENEMY BLOOD TO LIQUID GOLD.
"WIELDED SWIFTLY, I MIGHT DEFEAT MORDO WITH THIS... BEFORE SUCCUMBING TO RAVENOUS GREED AND PLUNGING THE BLADE INTO MY OWN GILDED HEART.
"THE NECKLACE OF BODIL WOULD, BELIEVE IT OR NOT, SUMMON A MASSIVE ARMY OF UNKILLABLE GHOST BEARS. NOT A BAD WAY TO GO...
"...SO LONG AS ONE OF US IS COMFORTABLE SPENDING ONE NIGHT A MONTH AS A STARK-RAVING MINDLESS HALF-URSINE WEREBEAR."

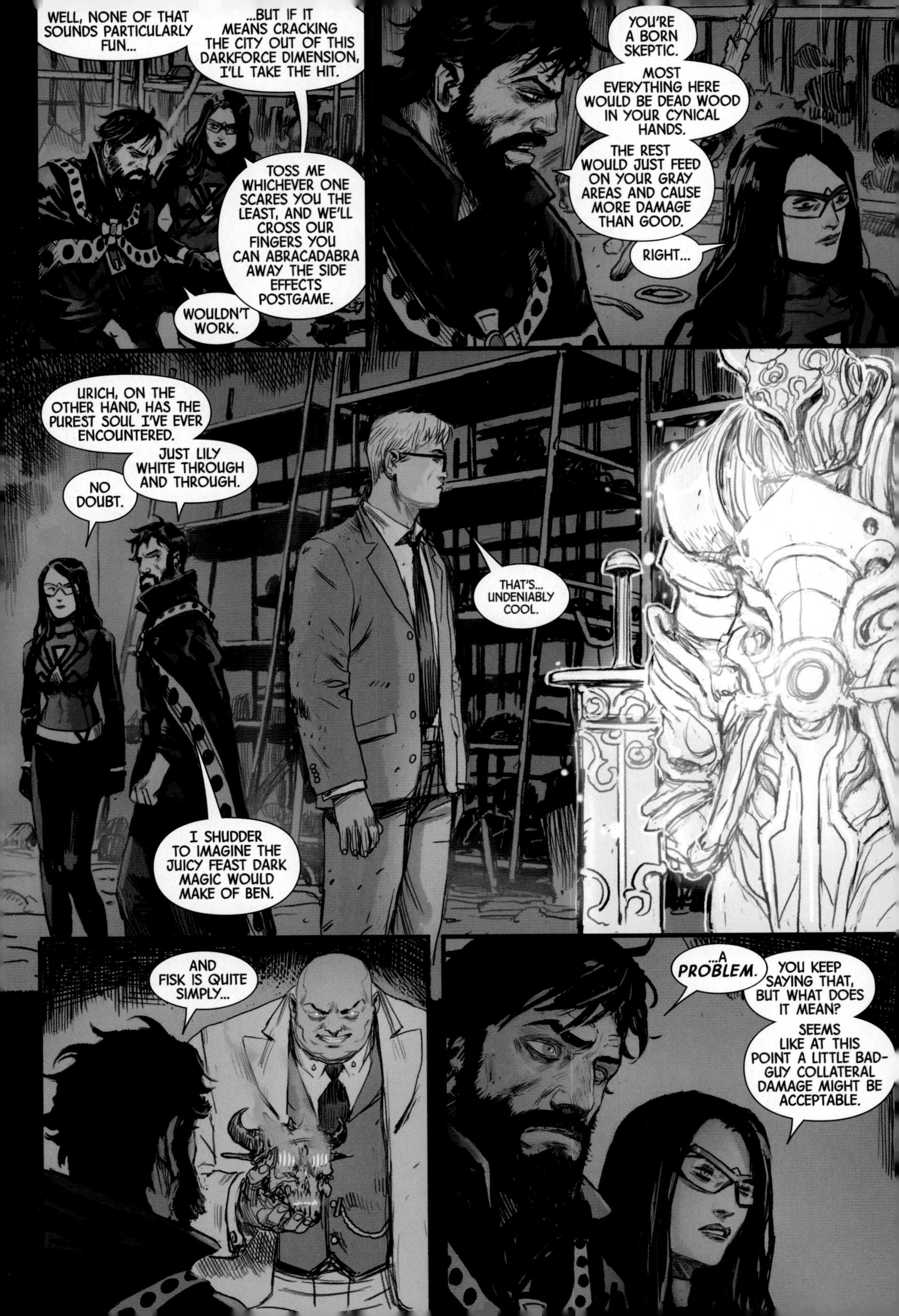

WELL, NONE OF THAT SOUNDS PARTICULARLY FUN...
...BUT IF IT MEANS CRACKING THE CITY OUT OF THIS DARKFORCE DIMENSION, I'LL TAKE THE HIT.
TOSS ME WHICHEVER ONE SCARES YOU THE LEAST, AND WE'LL CROSS OUR FINGERS YOU CAN ABRACADABRA AWAY THE SIDE EFFECTS POSTGAME.
WOULDN'T WORK.
YOU'RE A BORN SKEPTIC.
MOST EVERYTHING HERE WOULD BE DEAD WOOD IN YOUR CYNICAL HANDS.
THE REST WOULD JUST FEED ON YOUR GRAY AREAS AND CAUSE MORE DAMAGE THAN GOOD.
RIGHT...
URICH, ON THE OTHER HAND, HAS THE PUREST SOUL I'VE EVER ENCOUNTERED.
JUST LILY WHITE THROUGH AND THROUGH.
NO DOUBT.
THAT'S... UNDENIABLY COOL.
I SHUDDER TO IMAGINE THE JUICY FEAST DARK MAGIC WOULD MAKE OF BEN.
AND FISK IS QUITE SIMPLY...
...A PROBLEM.
YOU KEEP SAYING THAT, BUT WHAT DOES IT MEAN?
SEEMS LIKE AT THIS POINT A LITTLE BAD-GUY COLLATERAL DAMAGE MIGHT BE ACCEPTABLE.

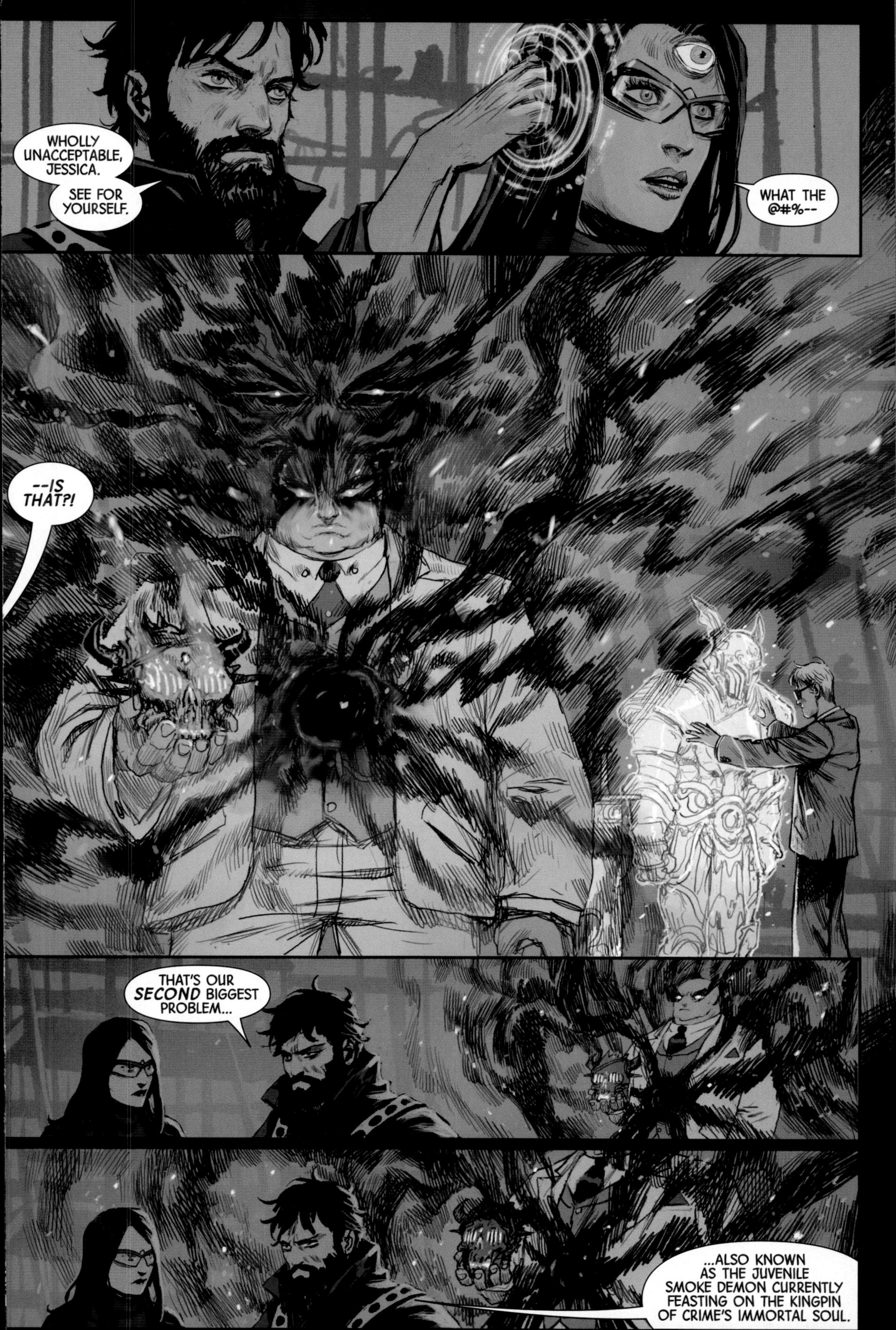
WHOLLY UNACCEPTABLE, JESSICA.
SEE FOR YOURSELF.
WHAT THE @#%--
--IS THAT?!
THAT'S OUR SECOND BIGGEST PROBLEM...
...ALSO KNOWN AS THE JUVENILE SMOKE DEMON CURRENTLY FEASTING ON THE KINGPIN OF CRIME'S IMMORTAL SOUL.

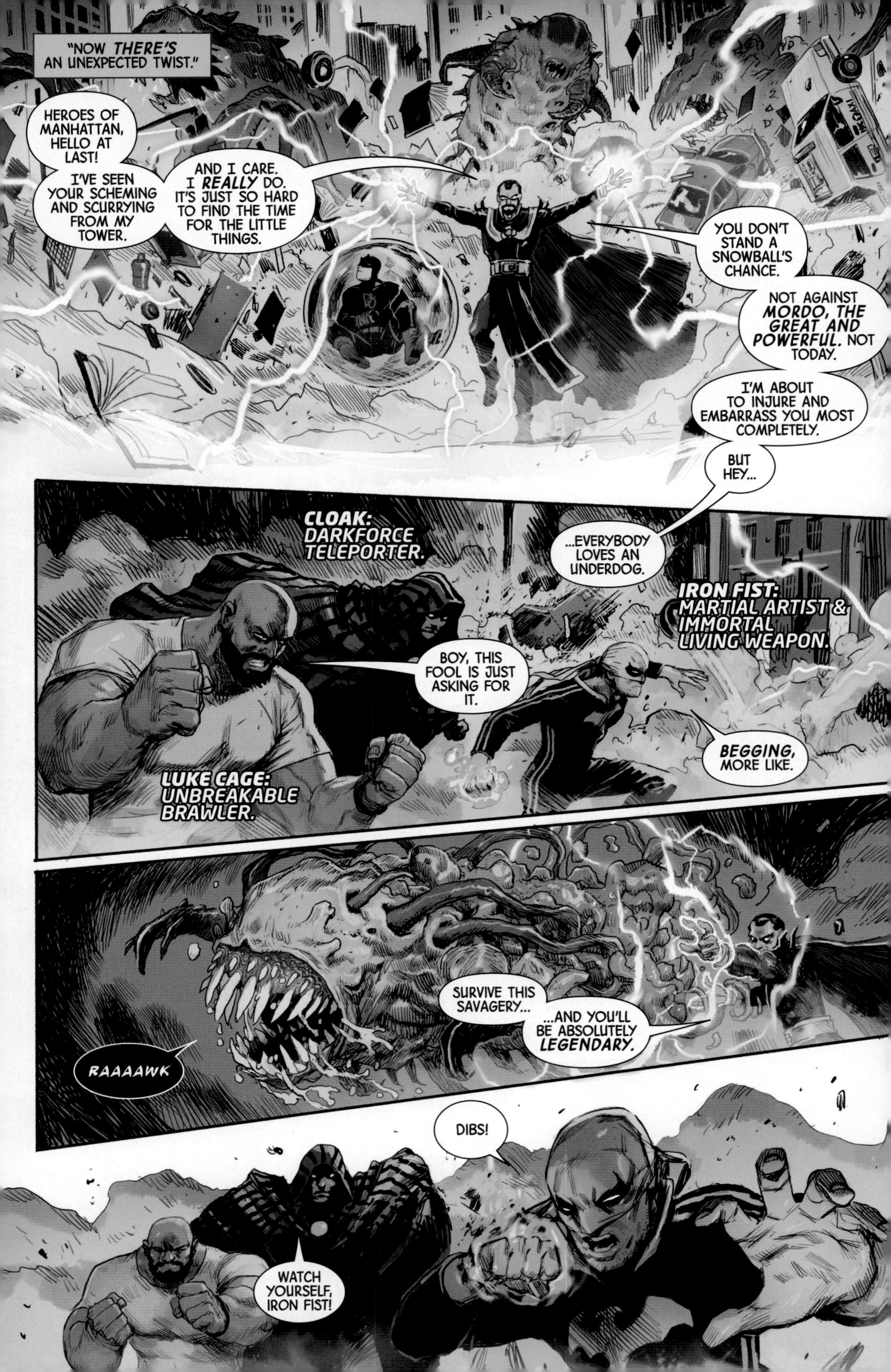

"NOW THERE'S AN UNEXPECTED TWIST."
HEROES OF MANHATTAN, HELLO AT LAST!
I'VE SEEN YOUR SCHEMING AND SCURRYING FROM MY TOWER.
AND I CARE. I REALLY DO. IT'S JUST SO HARD TO FIND THE TIME FOR THE LITTLE THINGS.
YOU DON'T STAND A SNOWBALL'S CHANCE.
NOT AGAINST MORDO, THE GREAT AND POWERFUL. NOT TODAY.
I'M ABOUT TO INJURE AND EMBARRASS YOU MOST COMPLETELY.
BUT HEY...
...EVERYBODY LOVES AN UNDERDOG.
CLOAK: DARKFORCE TELEPORTER.
IRON FIST: MARTIAL ARTIST & IMMORTAL LIVING WEAPON.
BOY, THIS FOOL IS JUST ASKING FOR IT.
BEGGING, MORE LIKE.
LUKE CAGE: UNBREAKABLE BRAWLER.
SURVIVE THIS SAVAGERY...
...AND YOU'LL BE ABSOLUTELY LEGENDARY.
RAAAAWK
DIBS!
WATCH YOURSELF, IRON FIST!

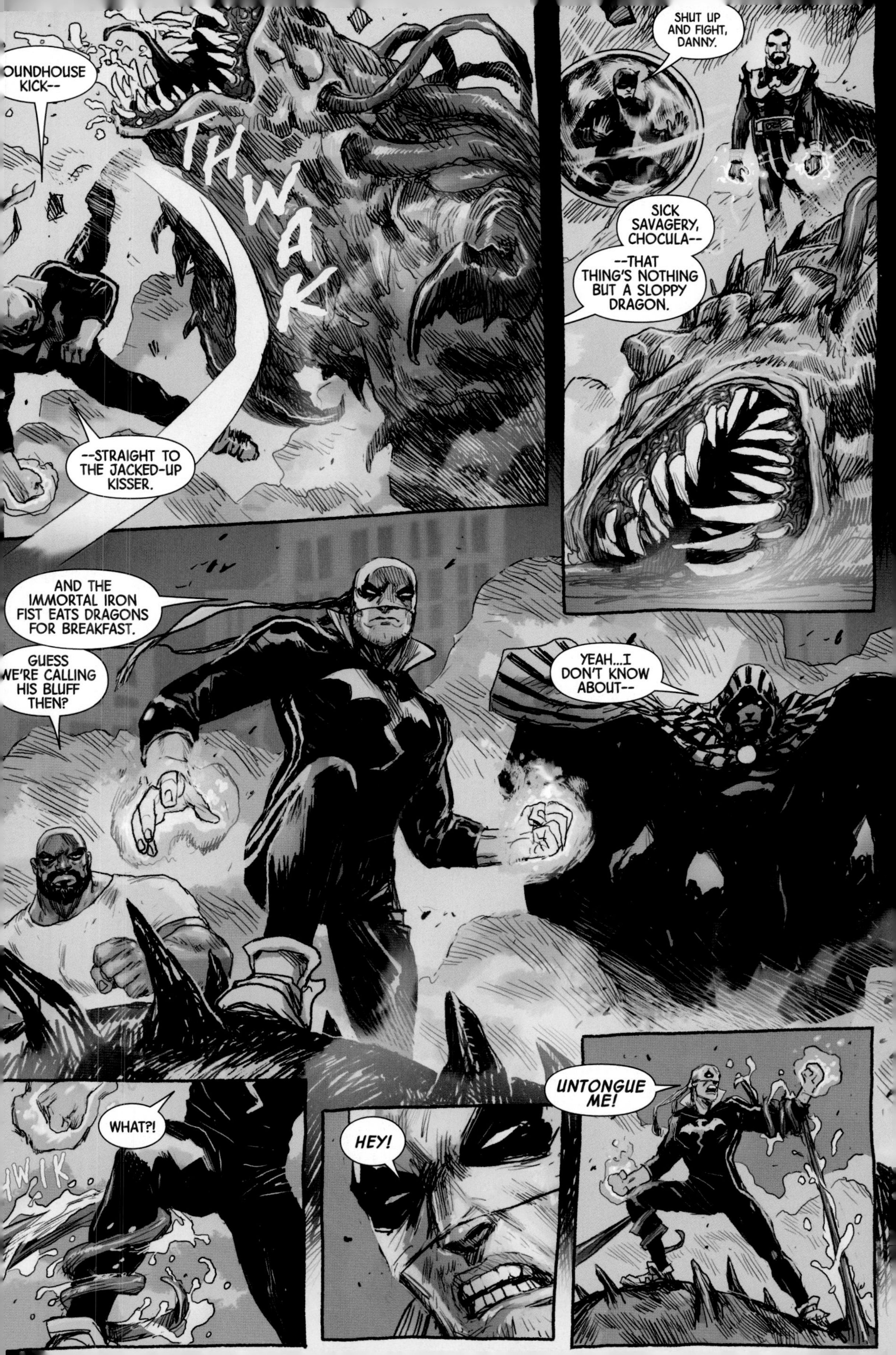
OUNDHOUSE KICK--
THWAK
--STRAIGHT TO THE JACKED-UP KISSER.
SHUT UP AND FIGHT, DANNY.
SICK SAVAGERY, CHOCULA--
--THAT THING'S NOTHING BUT A SLOPPY DRAGON.
AND THE IMMORTAL IRON FIST EATS DRAGONS FOR BREAKFAST.
GUESS WE'RE CALLING HIS BLUFF THEN?
YEAH...I DON'T KNOW ABOUT--
WHAT?!
HWIK
HEY!
UNTONGUE ME!

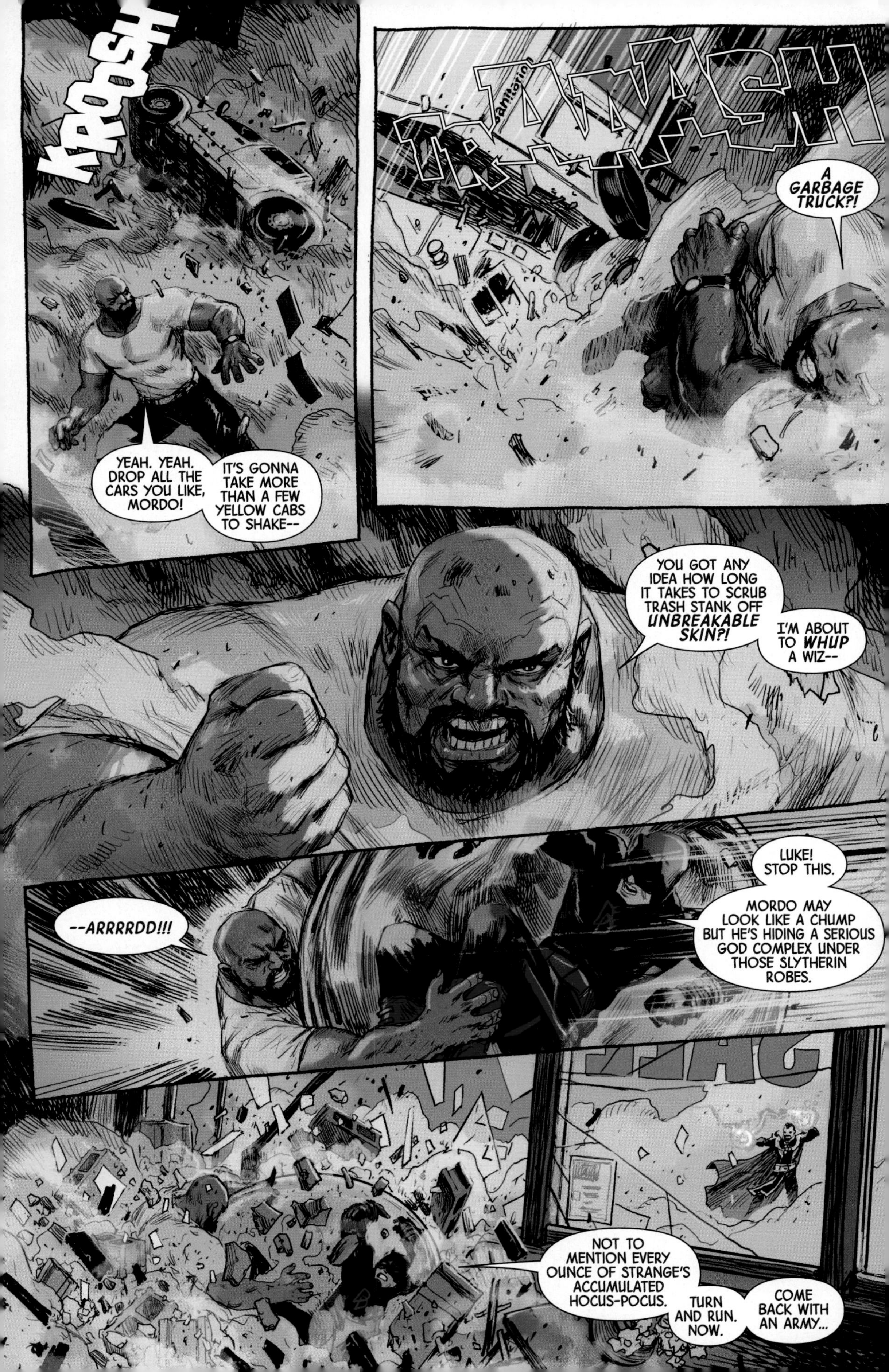
KROOSH
YEAH. YEAH. DROP ALL THE CARS YOU LIKE, MORDO!
IT'S GONNA TAKE MORE THAN A FEW YELLOW CABS TO SHAKE--
TRANNASH
A GARBAGE TRUCK?!
YOU GOT ANY IDEA HOW LONG IT TAKES TO SCRUB TRASH STANK OFF *UNBREAKABLE SKIN?!*
I'M ABOUT TO *WHUP* A WIZ--
--ARRRRDD!!!
LUKE! STOP THIS.
MORDO MAY LOOK LIKE A CHUMP BUT HE'S HIDING A SERIOUS GOD COMPLEX UNDER THOSE SLYTHERIN ROBES.
NOT TO MENTION EVERY OUNCE OF STRANGE'S ACCUMULATED HOCUS-POCUS.
TURN AND RUN. NOW.
COME BACK WITH AN ARMY...

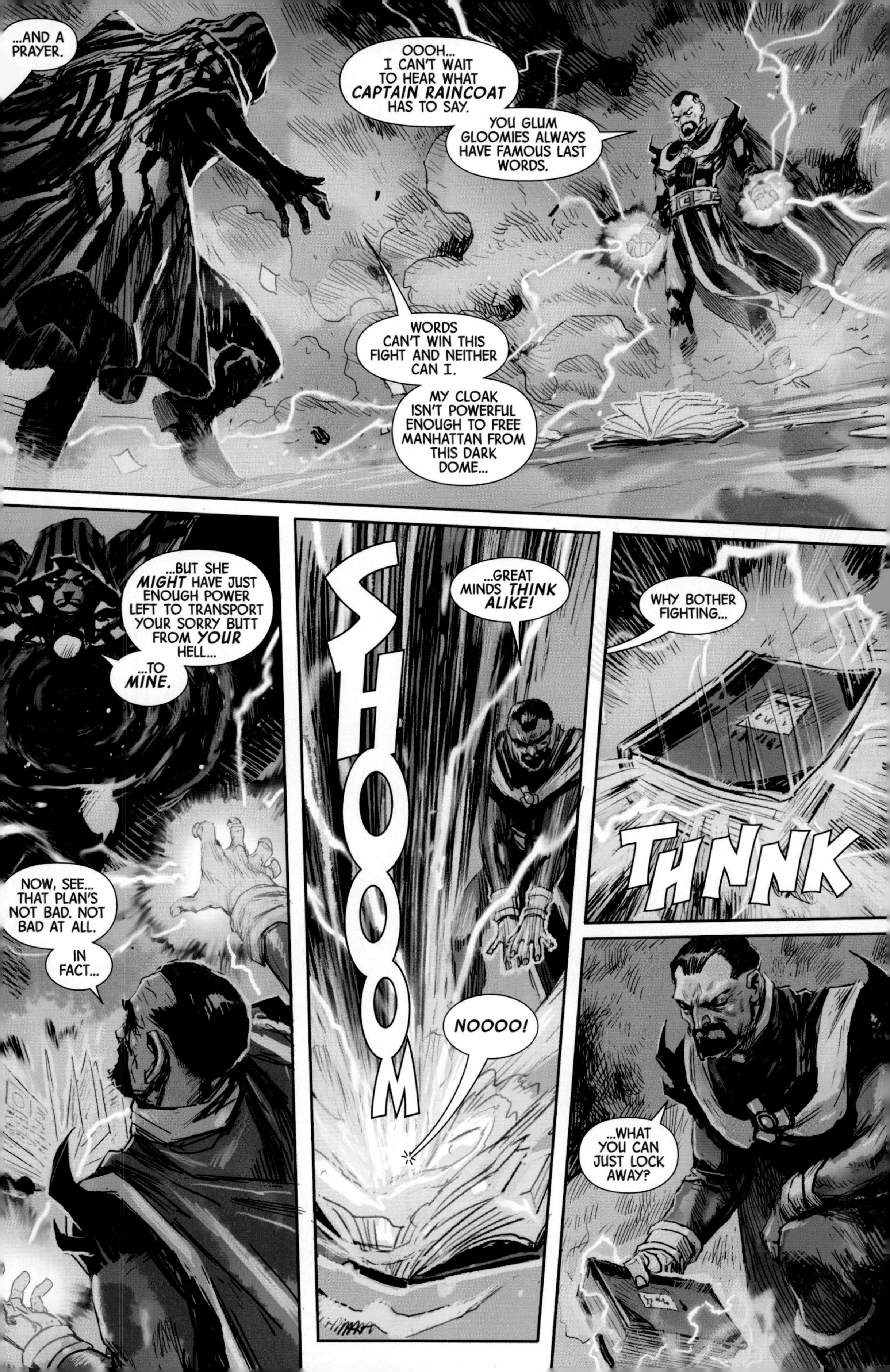
...AND A PRAYER.
OOOH... I CAN'T WAIT TO HEAR WHAT CAPTAIN RAINCOAT HAS TO SAY.
YOU GLUM GLOOMIES ALWAYS HAVE FAMOUS LAST WORDS.
WORDS CAN'T WIN THIS FIGHT AND NEITHER CAN I.
MY CLOAK ISN'T POWERFUL ENOUGH TO FREE MANHATTAN FROM THIS DARK DOME...
...BUT SHE MIGHT HAVE JUST ENOUGH POWER LEFT TO TRANSPORT YOUR SORRY BUTT FROM YOUR HELL...
...TO MINE.
NOW, SEE... THAT PLAN'S NOT BAD. NOT BAD AT ALL.
IN FACT...
SHOOOOM
...GREAT MINDS THINK ALIKE!
NOOOO!
WHY BOTHER FIGHTING...
THNNK
...WHAT YOU CAN JUST LOCK AWAY?

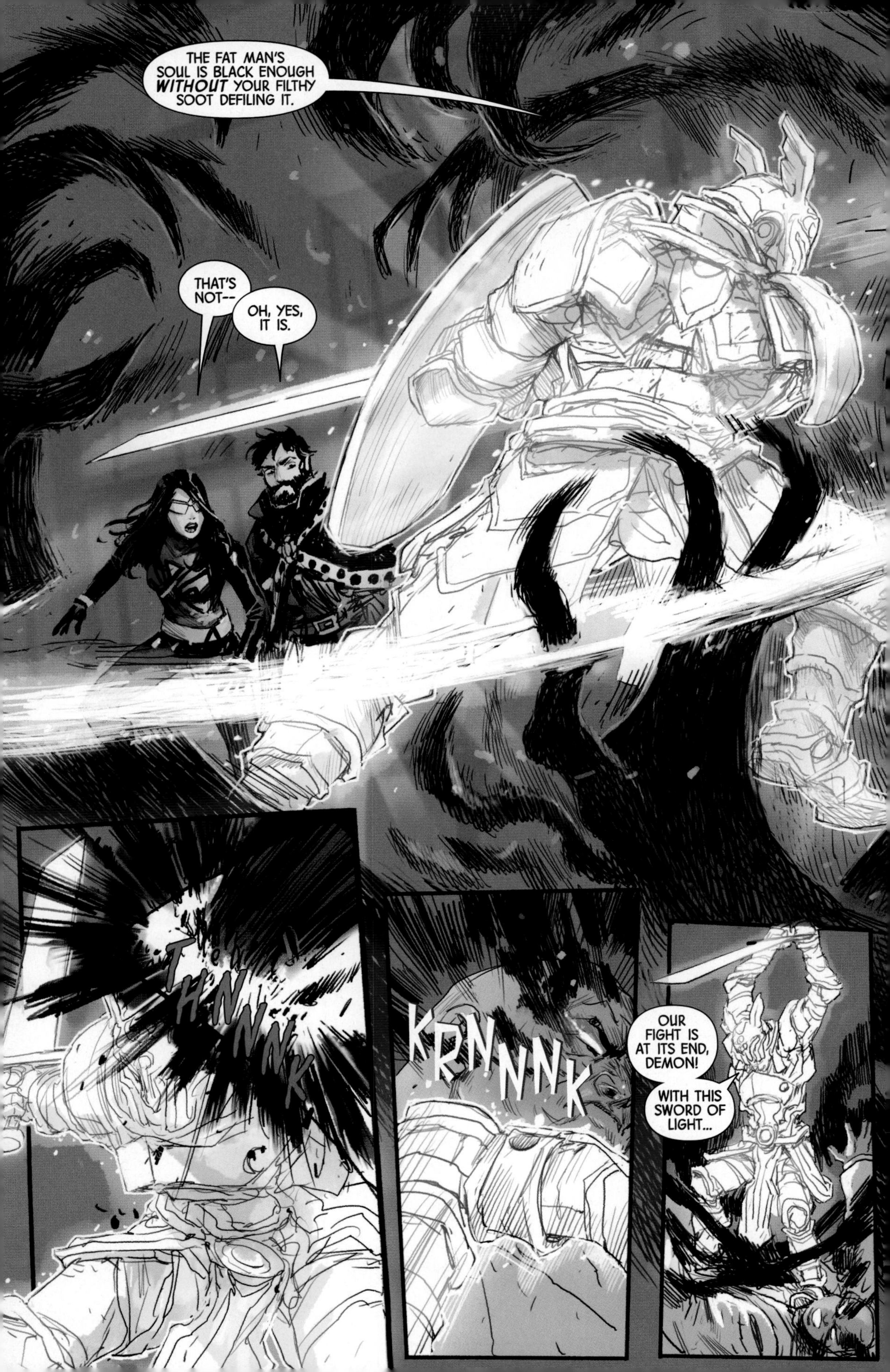
THE FAT MAN'S SOUL IS BLACK ENOUGH *WITHOUT* YOUR FILTHY SOOT DEFILING IT.
THAT'S NOT--
OH, YES, IT IS.
THHNNNK
KRNNNK
OUR FIGHT IS AT ITS END, DEMON!
WITH THIS SWORD OF LIGHT...

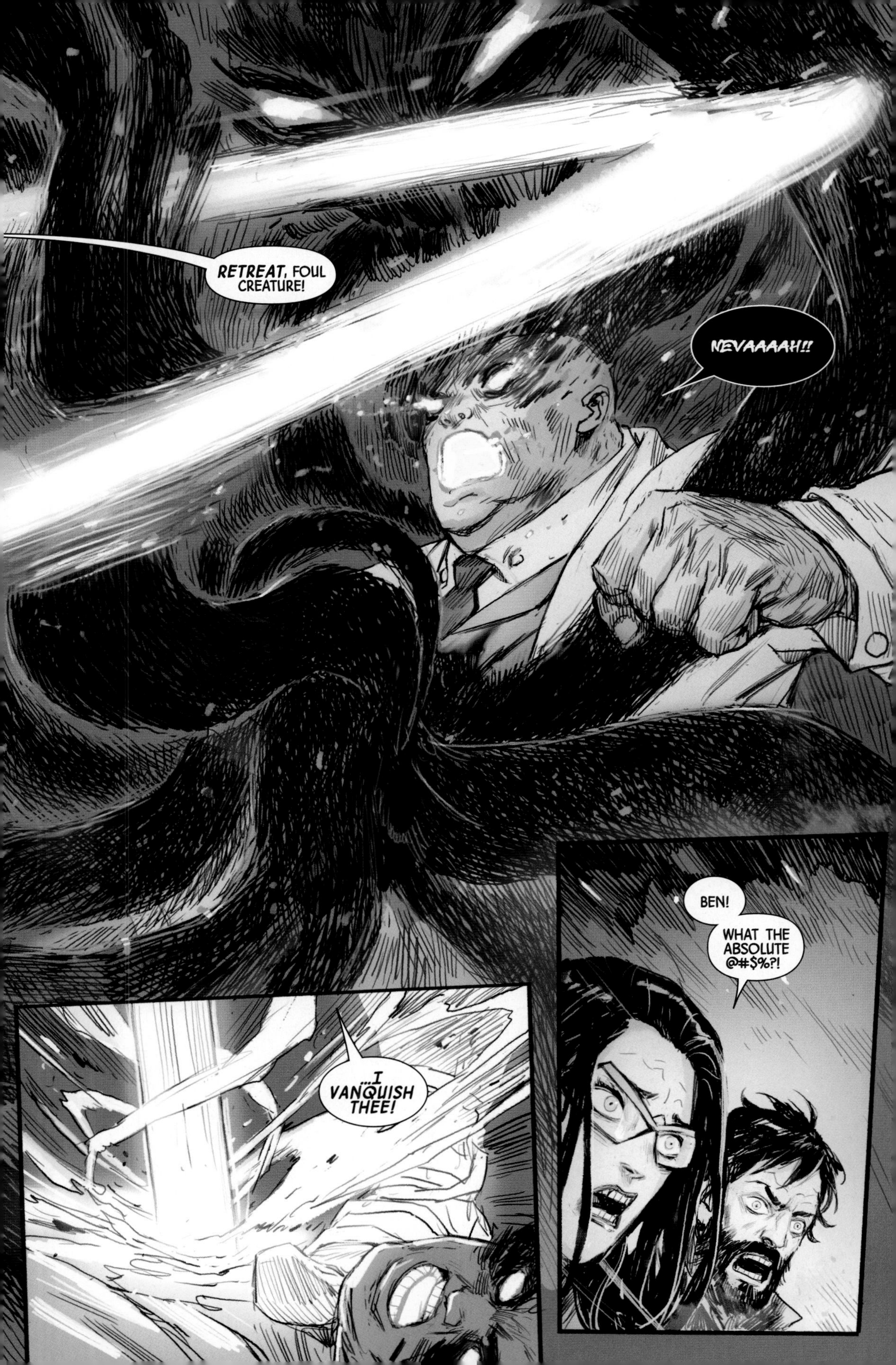

RETREAT, FOUL CREATURE!
NEVAAAAH!!
BEN!
WHAT THE ABSOLUTE @#$%?!
...I VANQUISH THEE!

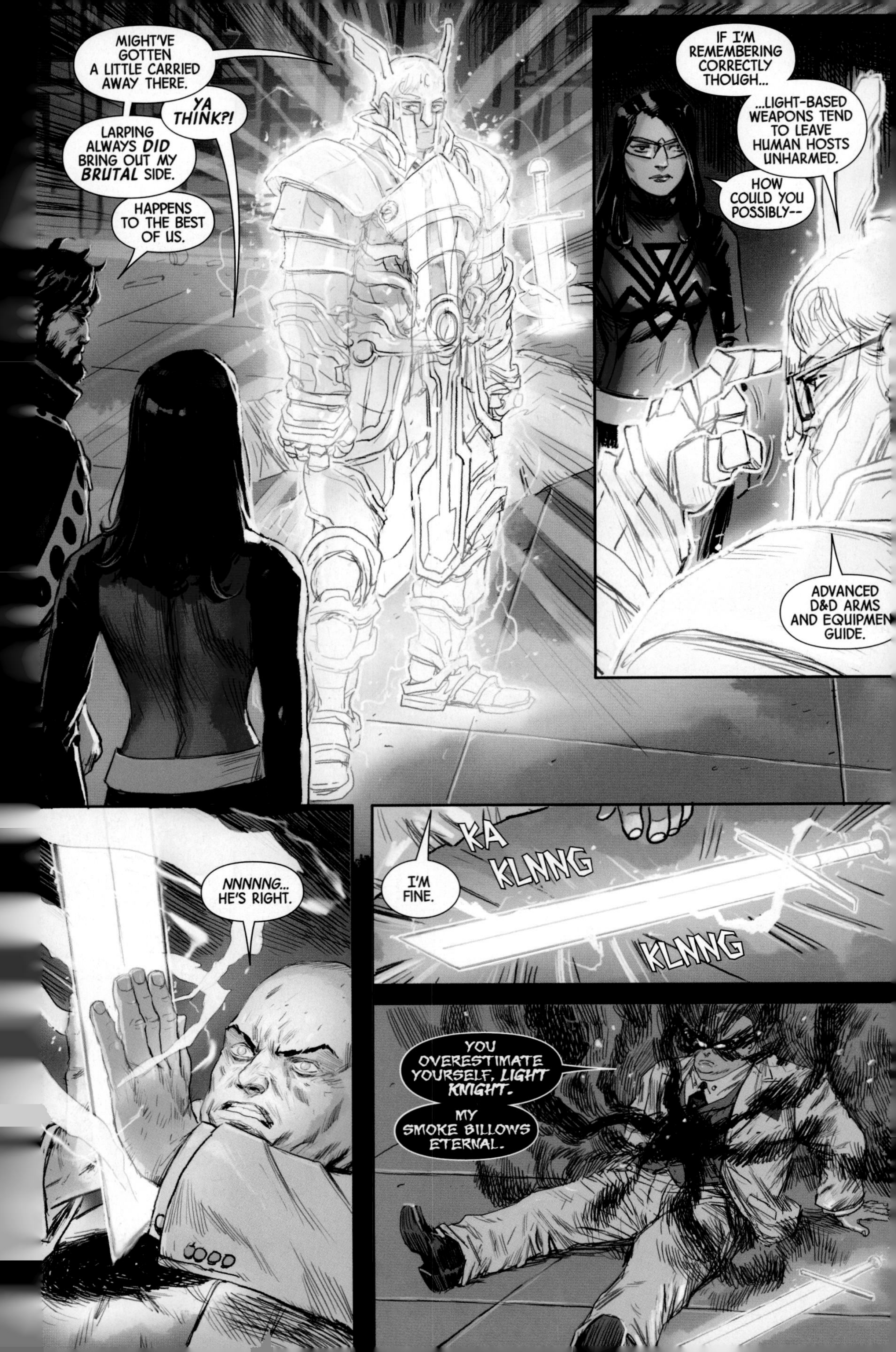
MIGHT'VE GOTTEN A LITTLE CARRIED AWAY THERE.
YA THINK?!
LARPING ALWAYS DID BRING OUT MY BRUTAL SIDE.
HAPPENS TO THE BEST OF US.
IF I'M REMEMBERING CORRECTLY THOUGH...
...LIGHT-BASED WEAPONS TEND TO LEAVE HUMAN HOSTS UNHARMED.
HOW COULD YOU POSSIBLY--
ADVANCED D&D ARMS AND EQUIPMEN GUIDE.
NNNNNG... HE'S RIGHT.
I'M FINE.
KA KLNNG
KLNNG
YOU OVERESTIMATE YOURSELF, LIGHT KNIGHT.
MY SMOKE BILLOWS ETERNAL.

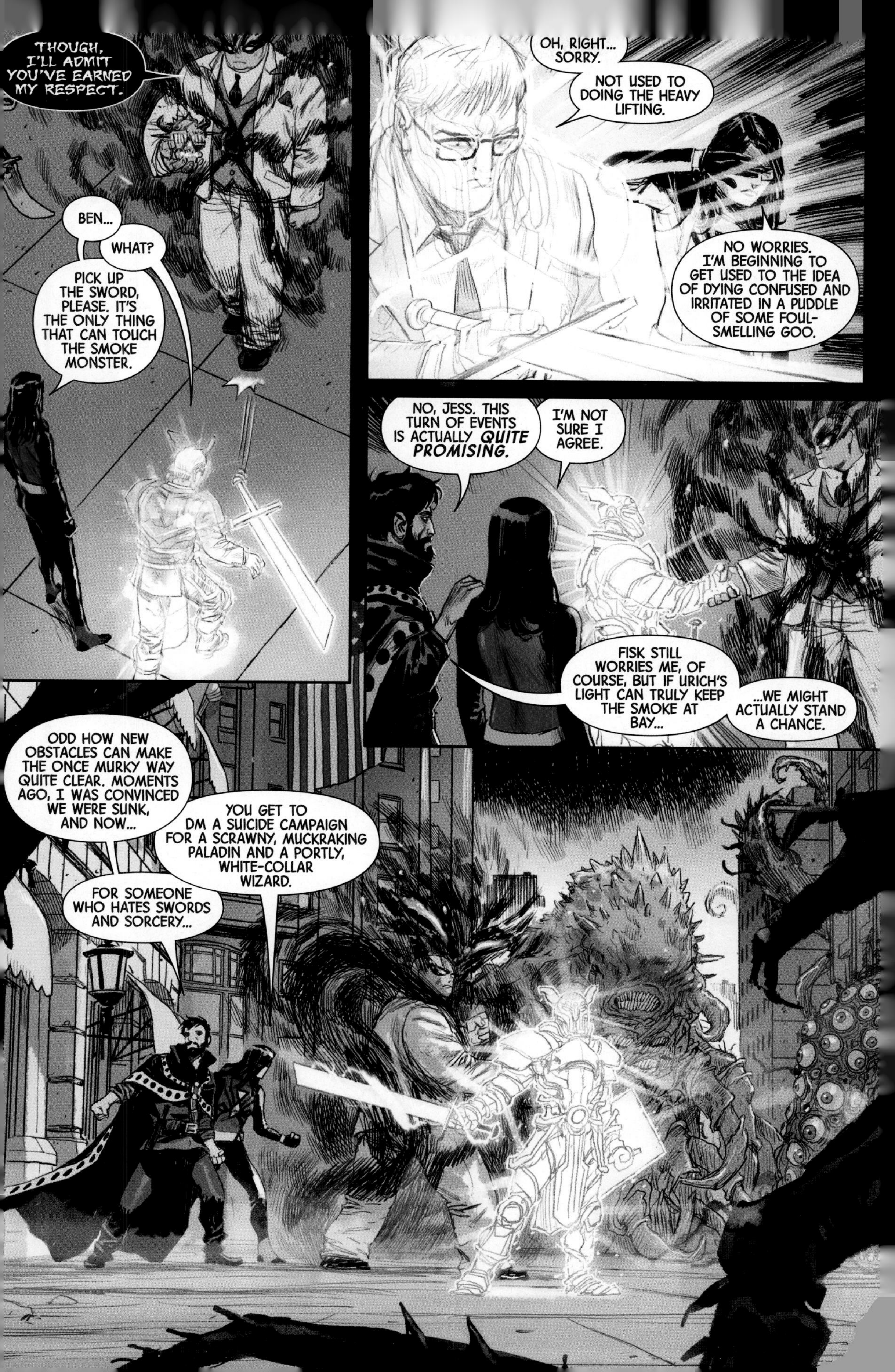
THOUGH, I'LL ADMIT YOU'VE EARNED MY RESPECT.
BEN...
WHAT?
PICK UP THE SWORD, PLEASE. IT'S THE ONLY THING THAT CAN TOUCH THE SMOKE MONSTER.
OH, RIGHT... SORRY.
NOT USED TO DOING THE HEAVY LIFTING.
NO WORRIES. I'M BEGINNING TO GET USED TO THE IDEA OF DYING CONFUSED AND IRRITATED IN A PUDDLE OF SOME FOUL-SMELLING GOO.
NO, JESS. THIS TURN OF EVENTS IS ACTUALLY *QUITE PROMISING.*
I'M NOT SURE I AGREE.
FISK STILL WORRIES ME, OF COURSE, BUT IF URICH'S LIGHT CAN TRULY KEEP THE SMOKE AT BAY...
...WE MIGHT ACTUALLY STAND A CHANCE.
ODD HOW NEW OBSTACLES CAN MAKE THE ONCE MURKY WAY QUITE CLEAR. MOMENTS AGO, I WAS CONVINCED WE WERE SUNK, AND NOW...
FOR SOMEONE WHO HATES SWORDS AND SORCERY...
YOU GET TO DM A SUICIDE CAMPAIGN FOR A SCRAWNY, MUCKRAKING PALADIN AND A PORTLY, WHITE-COLLAR WIZARD.

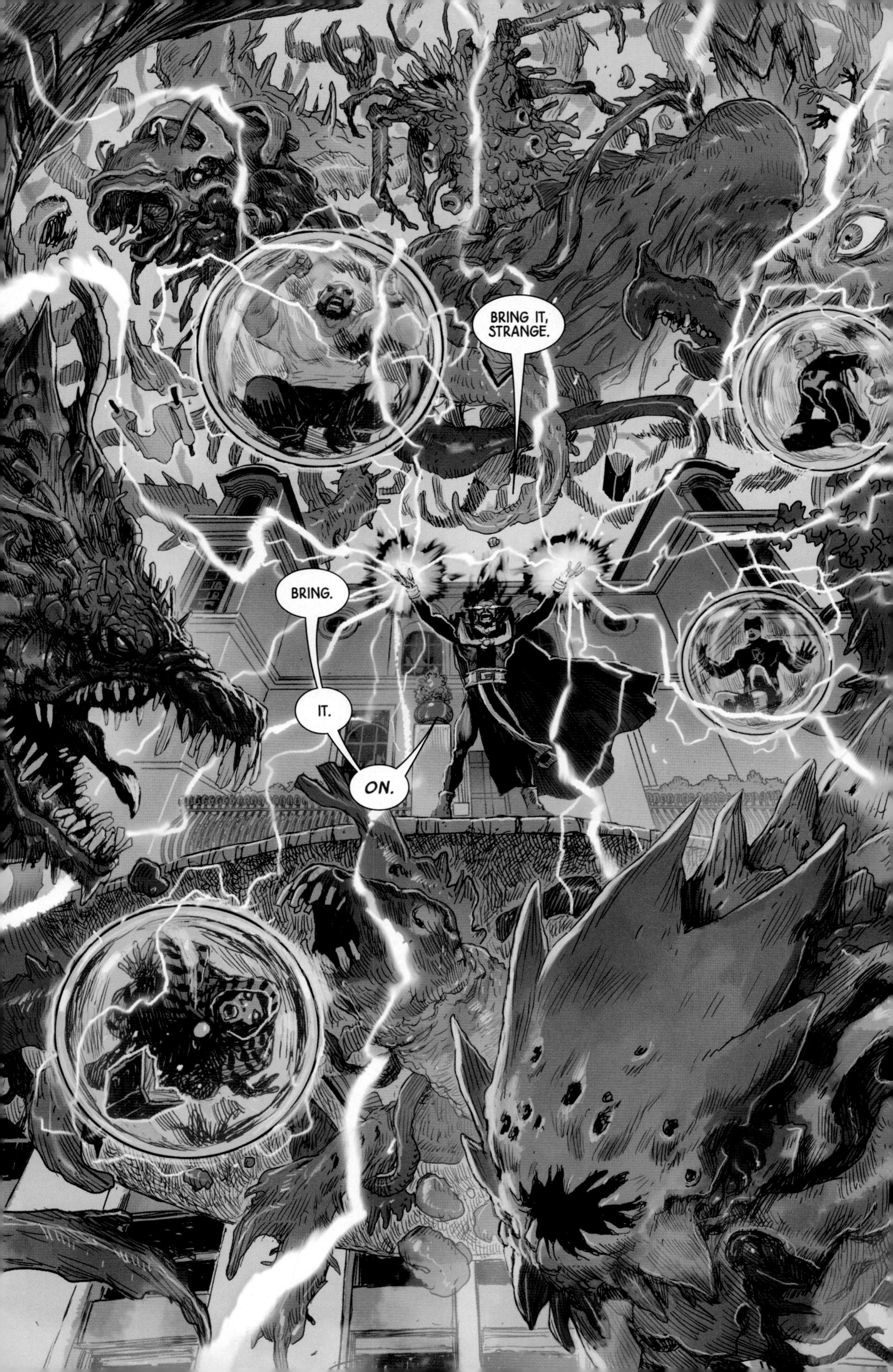
BRING IT, STRANGE.
BRING.
IT.
ON.

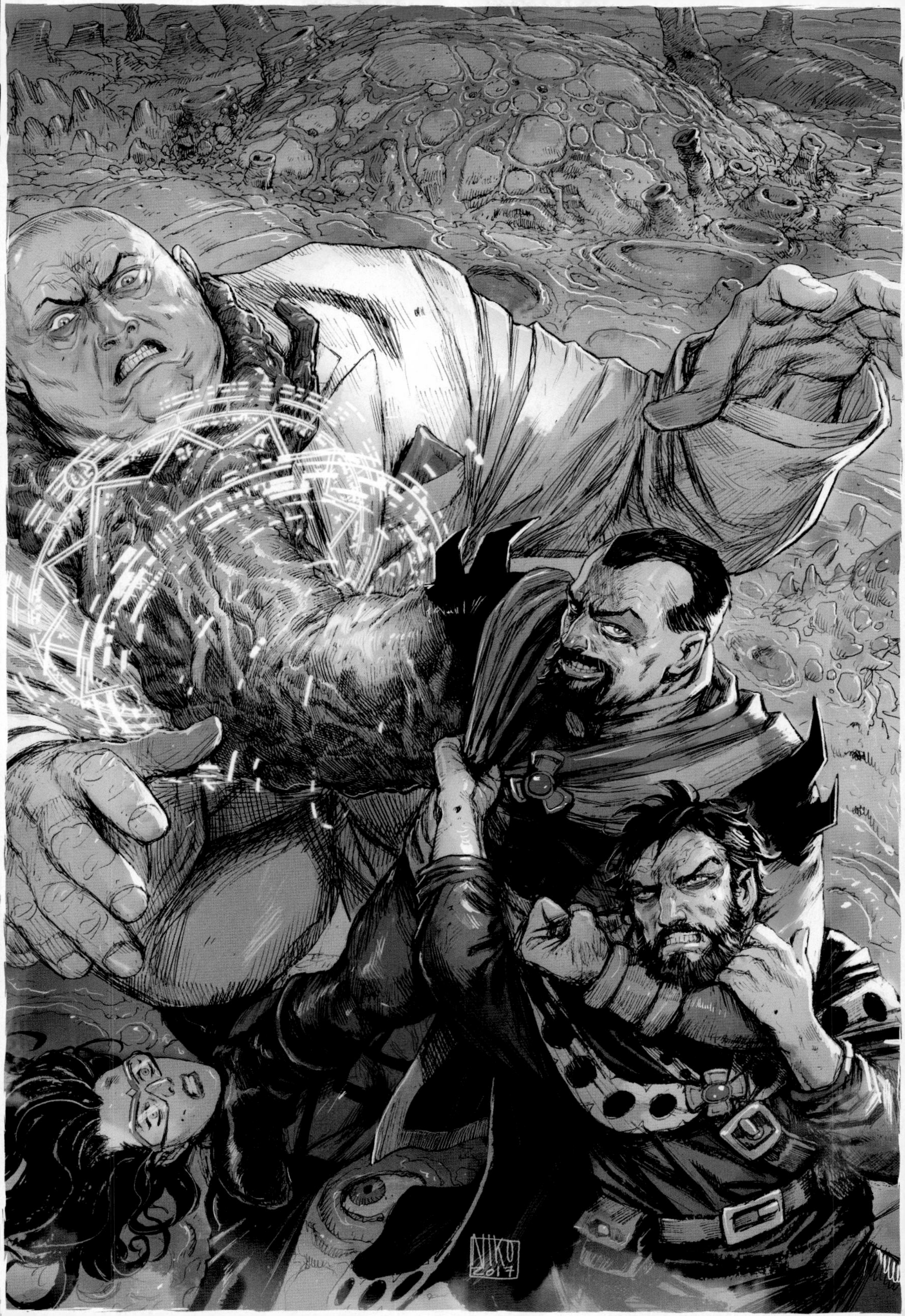
NIKO
2017

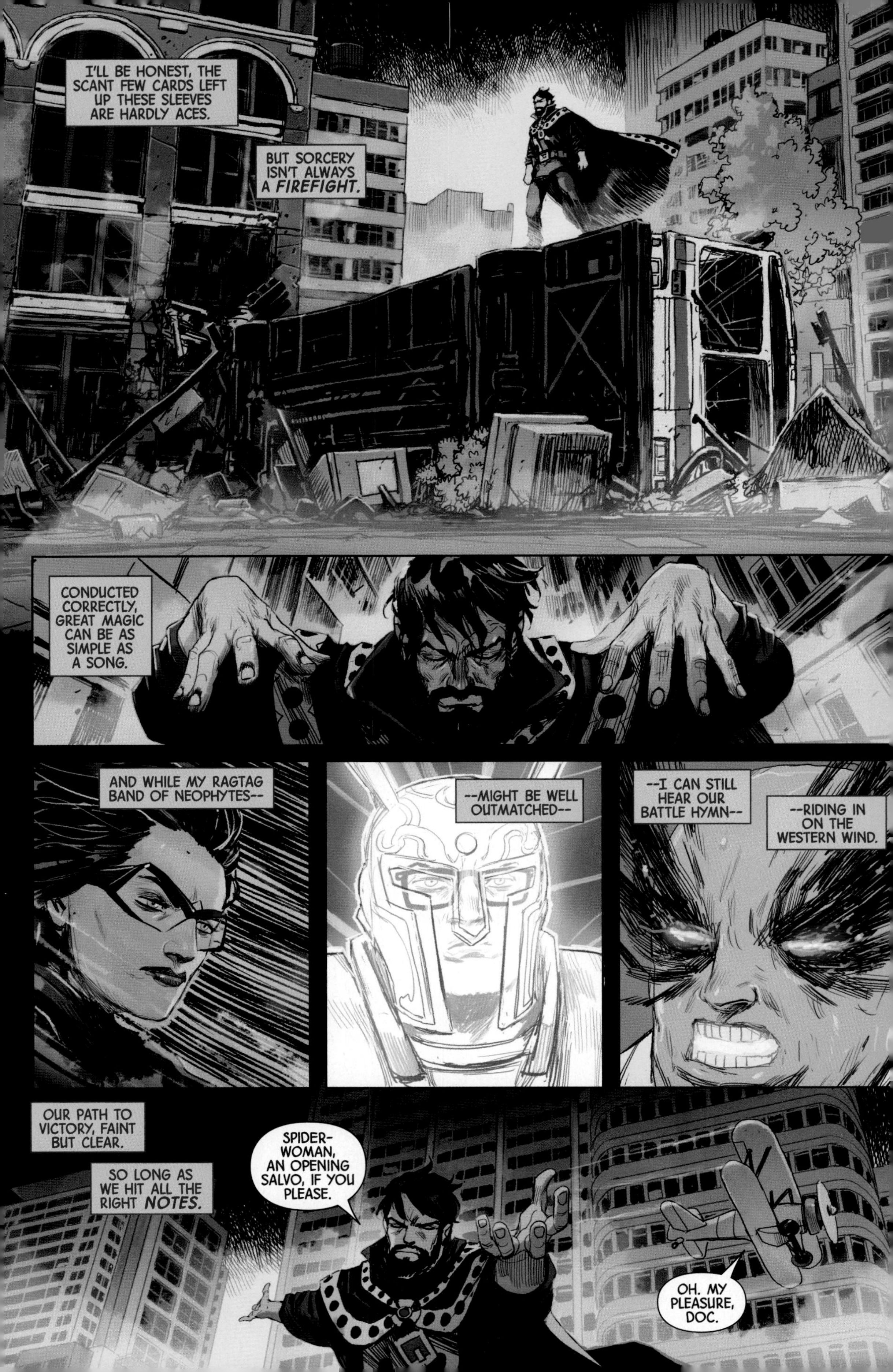
I'LL BE HONEST, THE SCANT FEW CARDS LEFT UP THESE SLEEVES ARE HARDLY ACES.
BUT SORCERY ISN'T ALWAYS A *FIREFIGHT*.
CONDUCTED CORRECTLY, GREAT MAGIC CAN BE AS SIMPLE AS A SONG.
AND WHILE MY RAGTAG BAND OF NEOPHYTES--
--MIGHT BE WELL OUTMATCHED--
--I CAN STILL HEAR OUR BATTLE HYMN--
--RIDING IN ON THE WESTERN WIND.
OUR PATH TO VICTORY, FAINT BUT CLEAR.
SO LONG AS WE HIT ALL THE RIGHT *NOTES*.
SPIDER-WOMAN, AN OPENING SALVO, IF YOU PLEASE.
OH. MY PLEASURE, DOC.

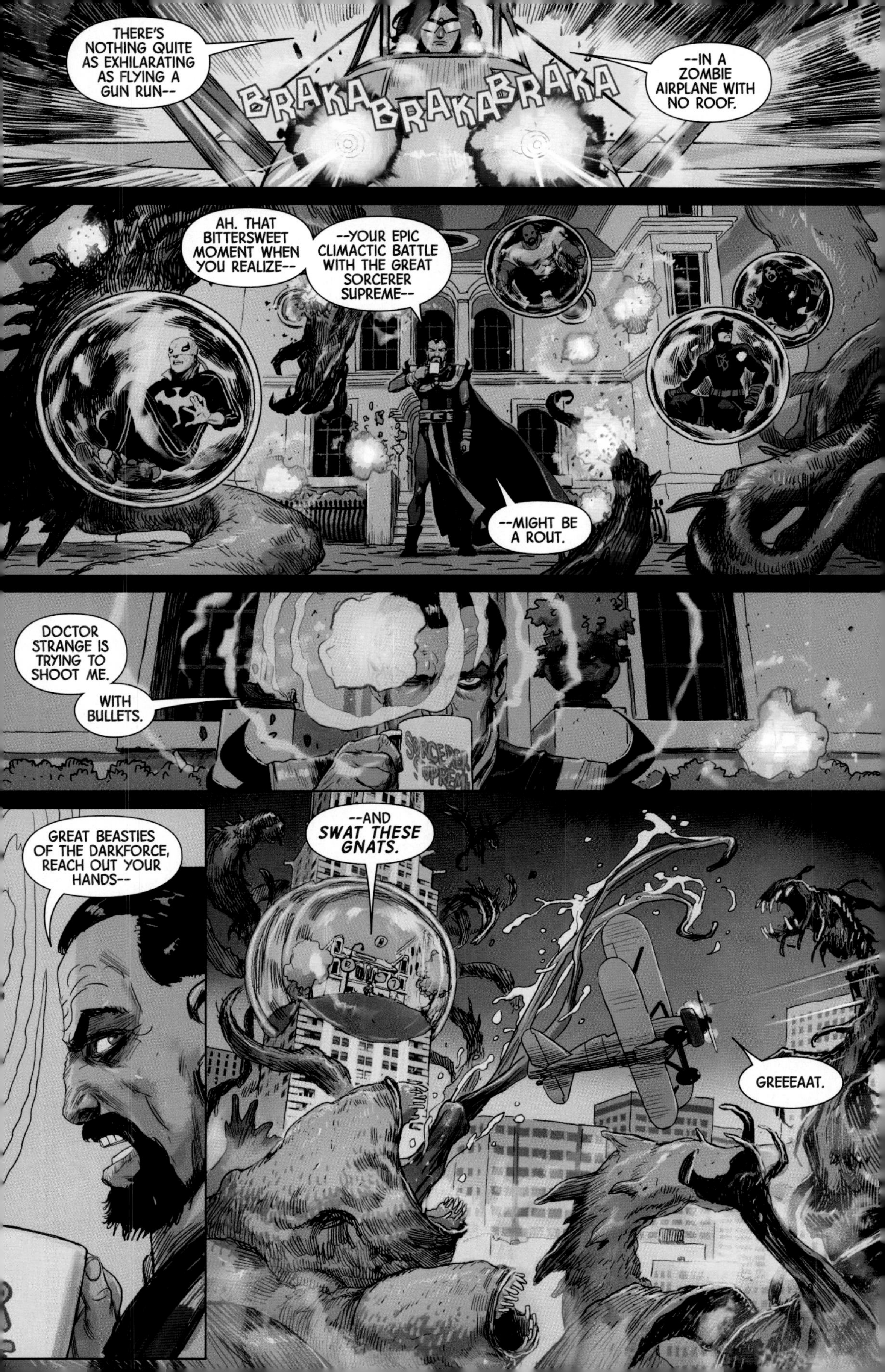
THERE'S NOTHING QUITE AS EXHILARATING AS FLYING A GUN RUN--
BRAKABRAKABRAKA
--IN A ZOMBIE AIRPLANE WITH NO ROOF.
AH. THAT BITTERSWEET MOMENT WHEN YOU REALIZE--
--YOUR EPIC CLIMACTIC BATTLE WITH THE GREAT SORCERER SUPREME--
--MIGHT BE A ROUT.
DOCTOR STRANGE IS TRYING TO SHOOT ME.
WITH BULLETS.
GREAT BEASTIES OF THE DARKFORCE, REACH OUT YOUR HANDS--
--AND SWAT THESE GNATS.
GREEEAAT.

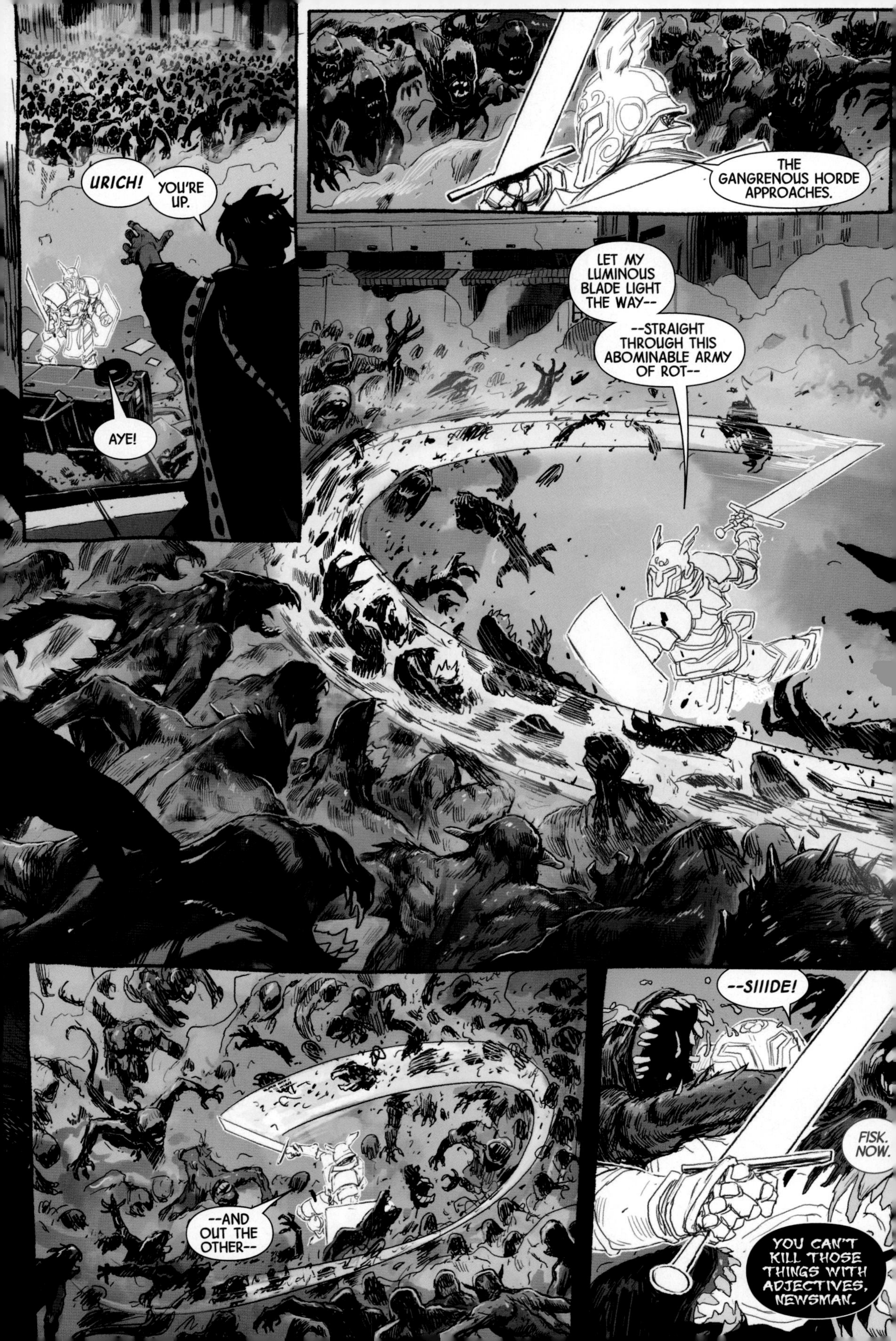
URICH!
YOU'RE UP.
AYE!
THE GANGRENOUS HORDE APPROACHES.
LET MY LUMINOUS BLADE LIGHT THE WAY--
--STRAIGHT THROUGH THIS ABOMINABLE ARMY OF ROT--
--AND OUT THE OTHER--
--SIIIDE!
FISK. NOW.
YOU CAN'T KILL THOSE THINGS WITH ADJECTIVES, NEWSMAN.

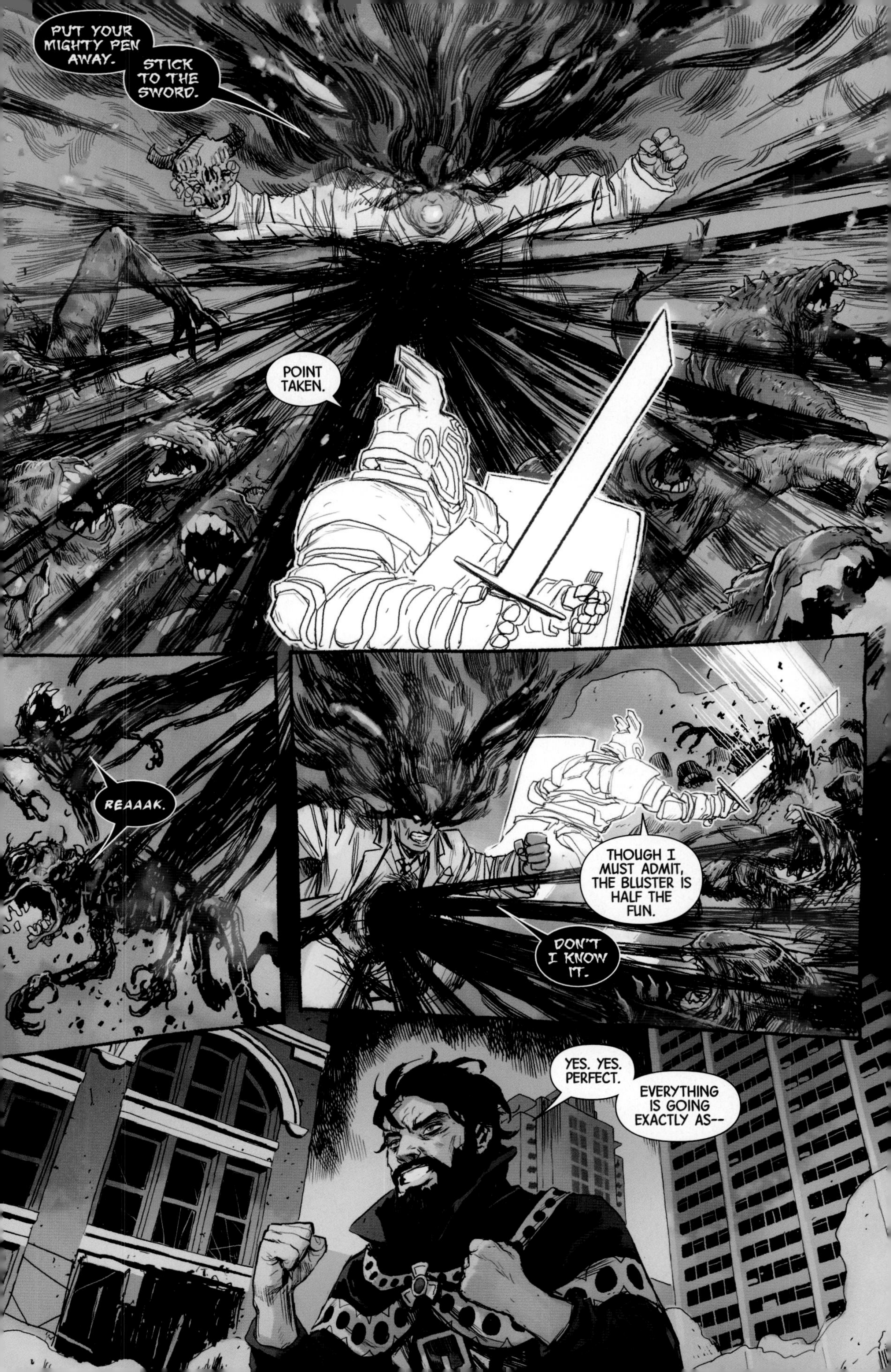
PUT YOUR MIGHTY PEN AWAY.
STICK TO THE SWORD.
POINT TAKEN.
REAAAK.
THOUGH I MUST ADMIT, THE BLUSTER IS HALF THE FUN.
DON'T I KNOW IT.
YES. YES. PERFECT.
EVERYTHING IS GOING EXACTLY AS--

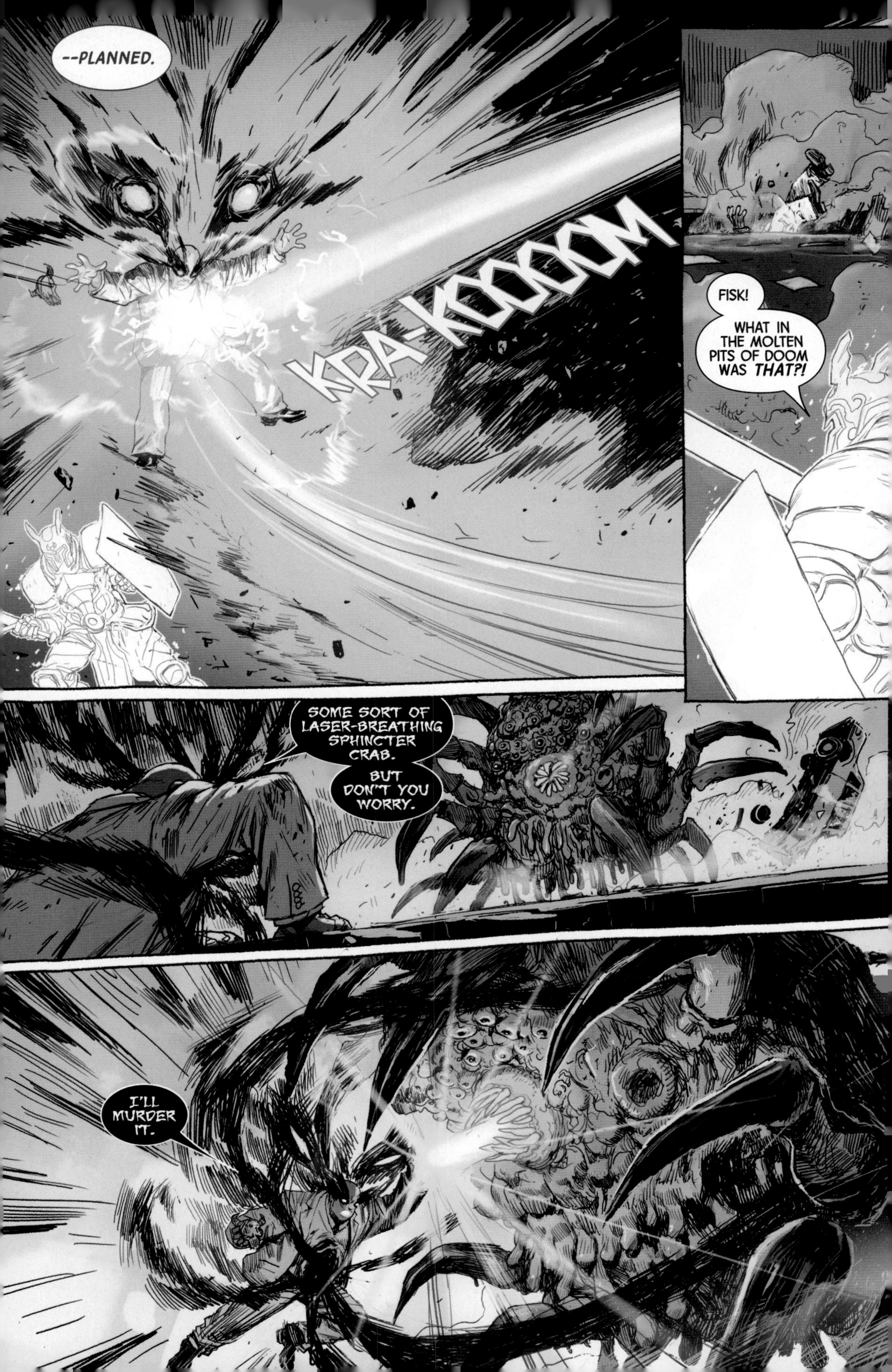
--PLANNED.
KRA-KOOOOOM
FISK!
WHAT IN THE MOLTEN PITS OF DOOM WAS THAT?!
SOME SORT OF LASER-BREATHING SPHINCTER CRAB.
BUT DON'T YOU WORRY.
I'LL MURDER IT.

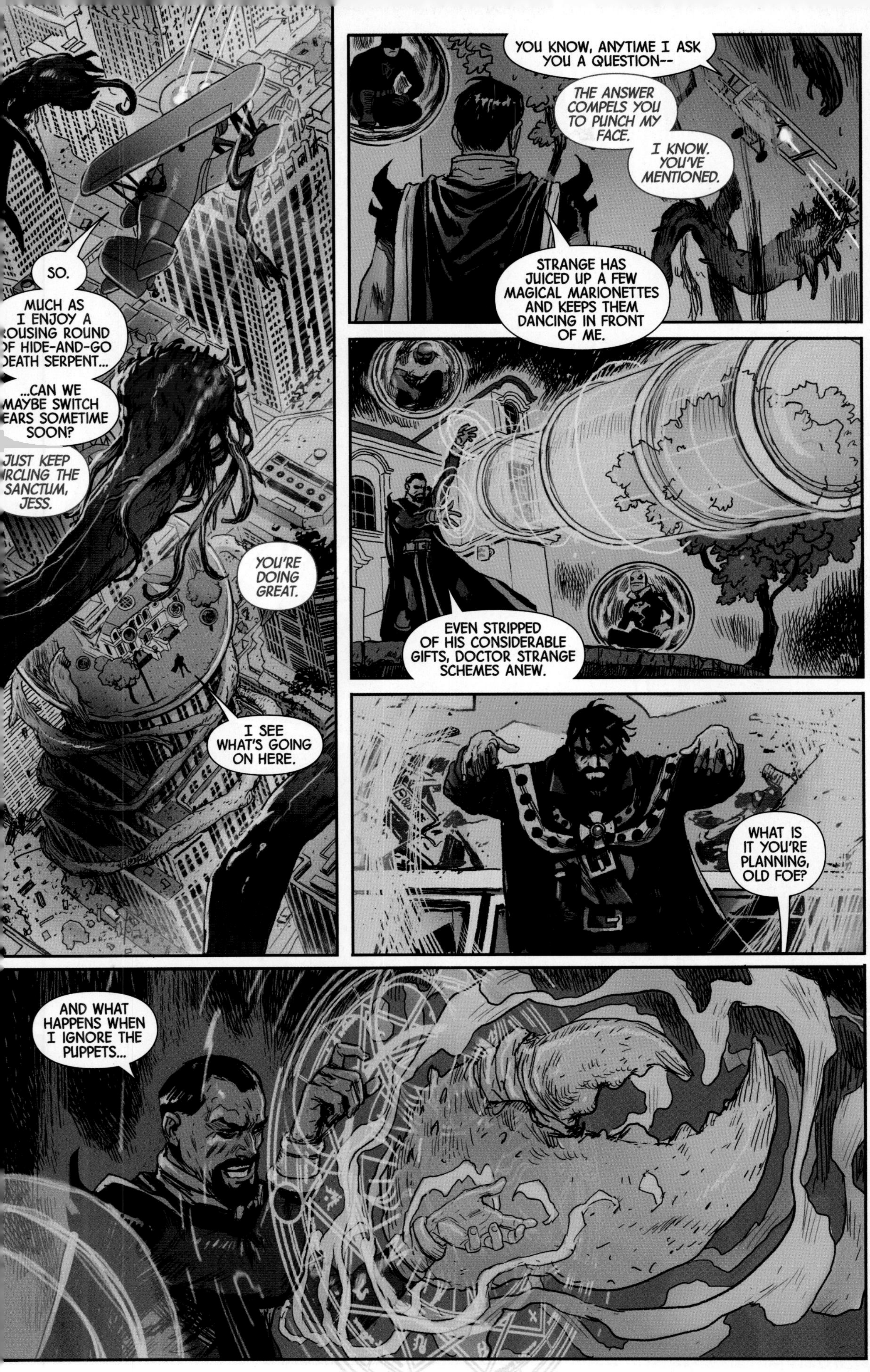
SO.
MUCH AS I ENJOY A ROUSING ROUND OF HIDE-AND-GO DEATH SERPENT...
...CAN WE MAYBE SWITCH GEARS SOMETIME SOON?
JUST KEEP CIRCLING THE SANCTUM, JESS.
YOU'RE DOING GREAT.
I SEE WHAT'S GOING ON HERE.
YOU KNOW, ANYTIME I ASK YOU A QUESTION--
THE ANSWER COMPELS YOU TO PUNCH MY FACE.
I KNOW. YOU'VE MENTIONED.
STRANGE HAS JUICED UP A FEW MAGICAL MARIONETTES AND KEEPS THEM DANCING IN FRONT OF ME.
EVEN STRIPPED OF HIS CONSIDERABLE GIFTS, DOCTOR STRANGE SCHEMES ANEW.
WHAT IS IT YOU'RE PLANNING, OLD FOE?
AND WHAT HAPPENS WHEN I IGNORE THE PUPPETS...

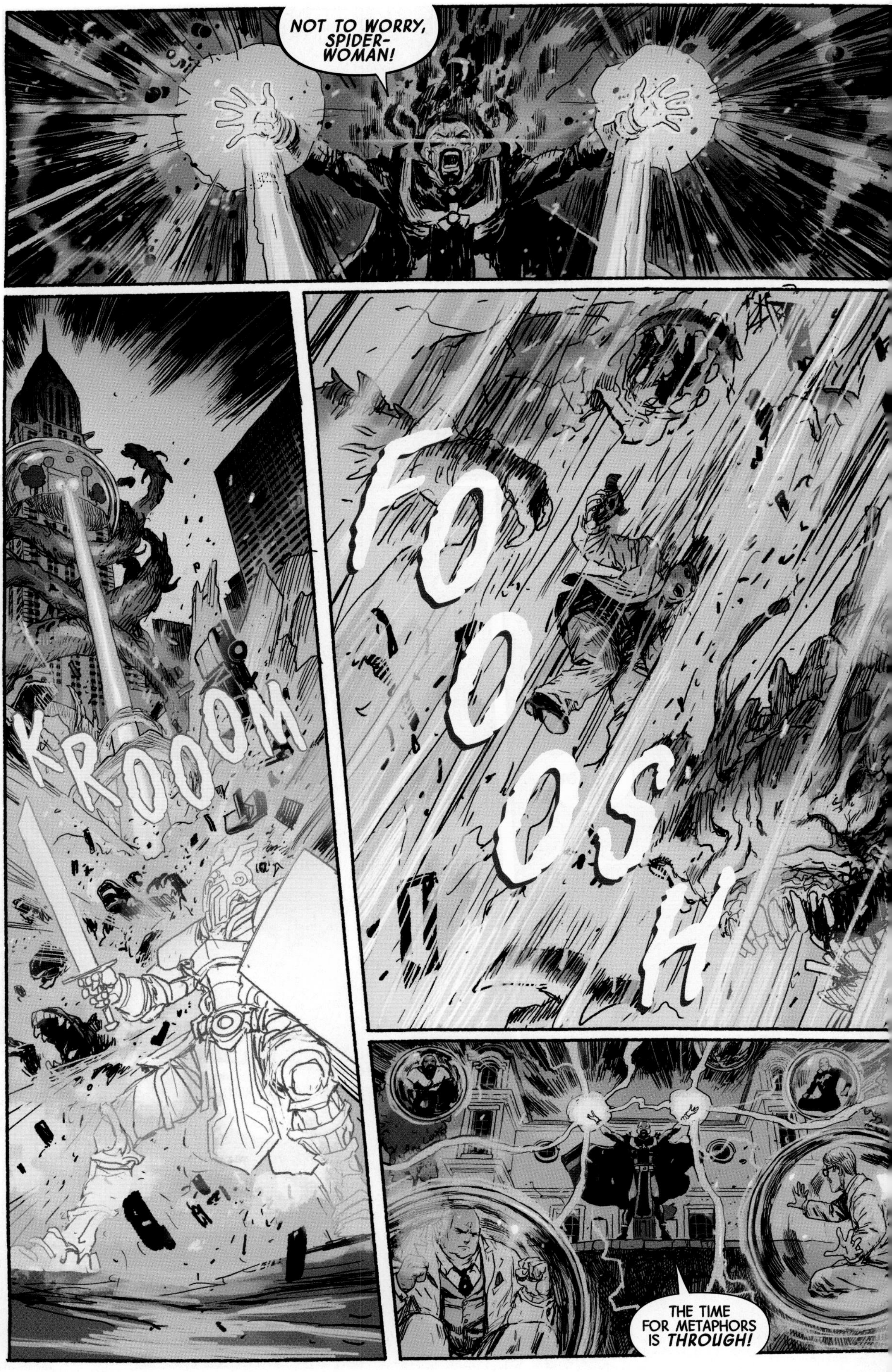
NOT TO WORRY, SPIDER-WOMAN!
KROOOM
FOOOOSH
THE TIME FOR METAPHORS IS THROUGH!

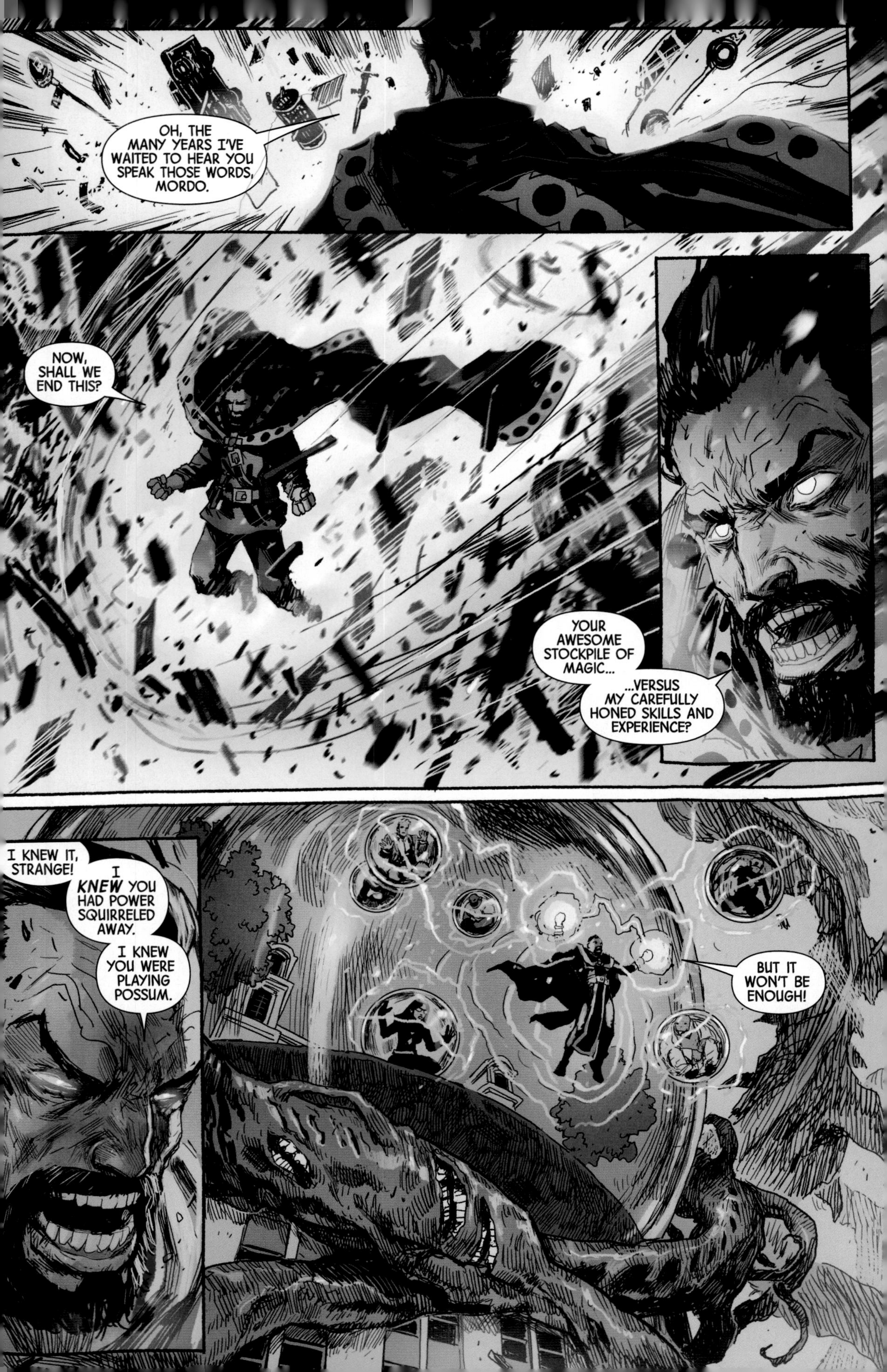
OH, THE MANY YEARS I'VE WAITED TO HEAR YOU SPEAK THOSE WORDS, MORDO.
NOW, SHALL WE END THIS?
YOUR AWESOME STOCKPILE OF MAGIC...
...VERSUS MY CAREFULLY HONED SKILLS AND EXPERIENCE?
I KNEW IT, STRANGE!
I *KNEW* YOU HAD POWER SQUIRRELED AWAY.
I KNEW YOU WERE PLAYING POSSUM.
BUT IT WON'T BE ENOUGH!

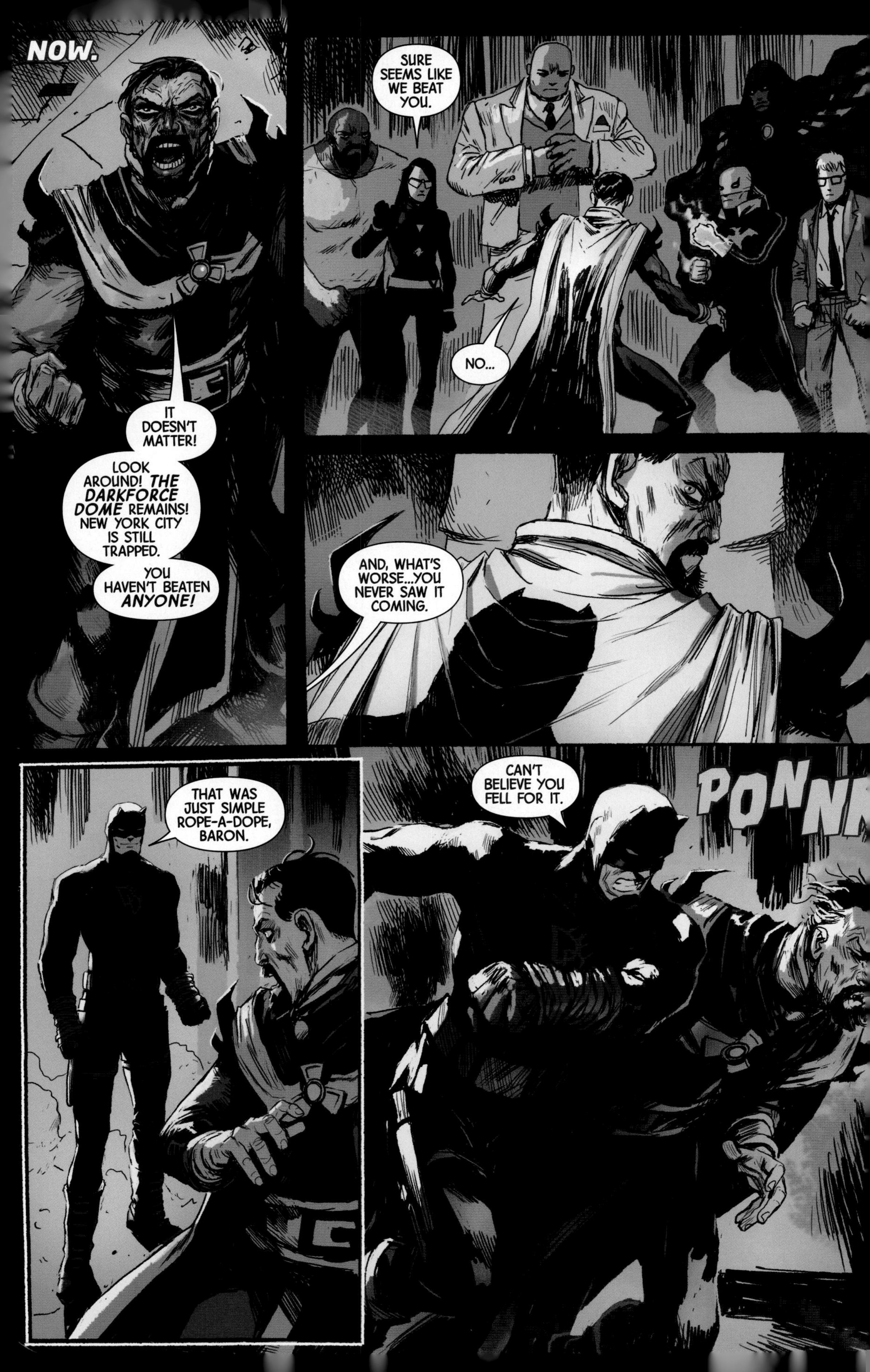
NOW.
SURE SEEMS LIKE WE BEAT YOU.
NO...
IT DOESN'T MATTER!
LOOK AROUND! THE DARKFORCE DOME REMAINS! NEW YORK CITY IS STILL TRAPPED.
YOU HAVEN'T BEATEN ANYONE!
AND, WHAT'S WORSE...YOU NEVER SAW IT COMING.
THAT WAS JUST SIMPLE ROPE-A-DOPE, BARON.
CAN'T BELIEVE YOU FELL FOR IT.
PONNN

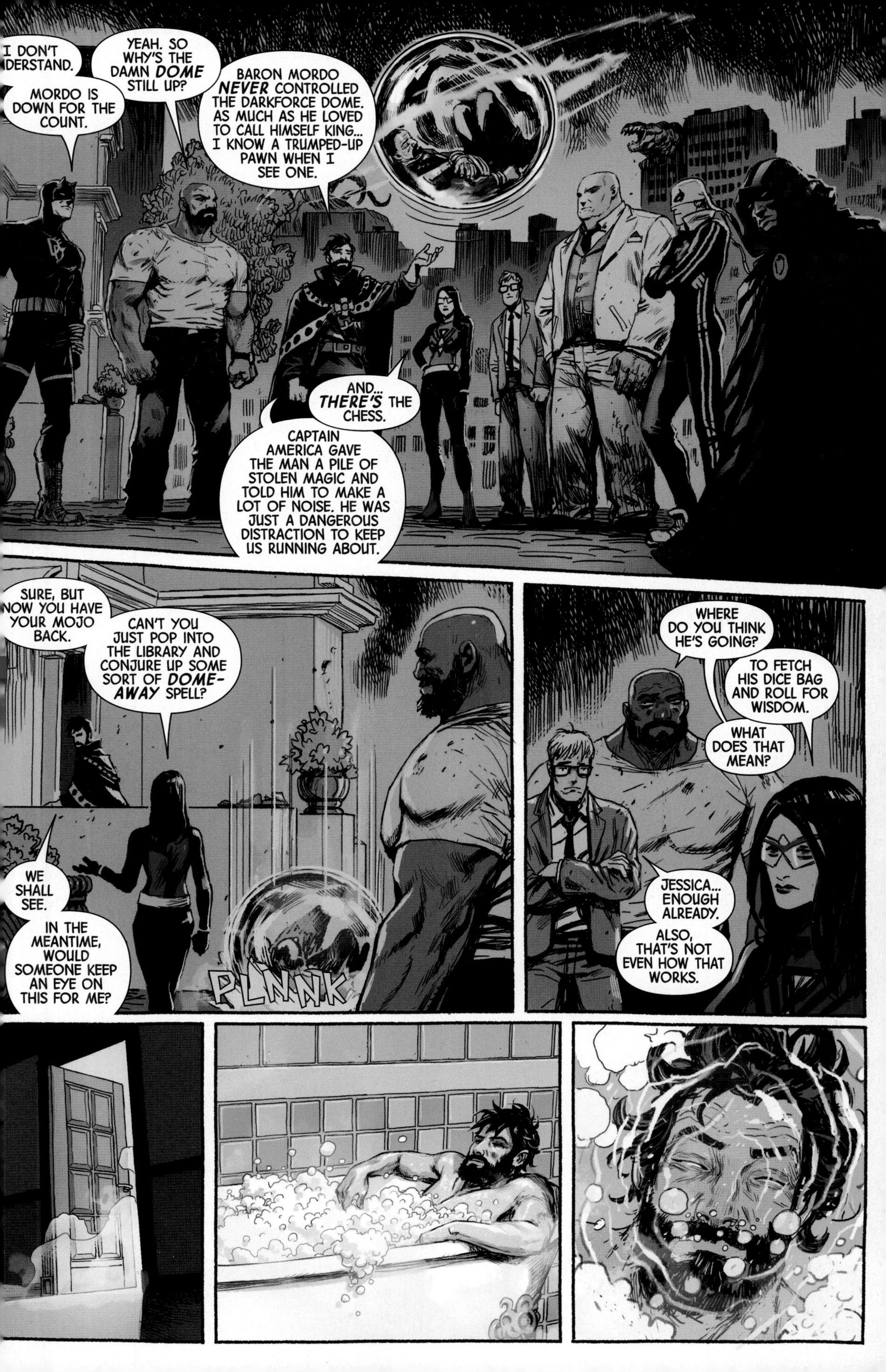
I DON'T
DERSTAND.
MORDO IS DOWN FOR THE COUNT.
YEAH. SO WHY'S THE DAMN DOME STILL UP?
BARON MORDO NEVER CONTROLLED THE DARKFORCE DOME. AS MUCH AS HE LOVED TO CALL HIMSELF KING... I KNOW A TRUMPED-UP PAWN WHEN I SEE ONE.
AND... THERE'S THE CHESS.
CAPTAIN AMERICA GAVE THE MAN A PILE OF STOLEN MAGIC AND TOLD HIM TO MAKE A LOT OF NOISE. HE WAS JUST A DANGEROUS DISTRACTION TO KEEP US RUNNING ABOUT.
SURE, BUT NOW YOU HAVE YOUR MOJO BACK.
CAN'T YOU JUST POP INTO THE LIBRARY AND CONJURE UP SOME SORT OF DOME-AWAY SPELL?
WE SHALL SEE.
IN THE MEANTIME, WOULD SOMEONE KEEP AN EYE ON THIS FOR ME?
PLNNK
WHERE DO YOU THINK HE'S GOING?
TO FETCH HIS DICE BAG AND ROLL FOR WISDOM.
WHAT DOES THAT MEAN?
JESSICA... ENOUGH ALREADY.
ALSO, THAT'S NOT EVEN HOW THAT WORKS.

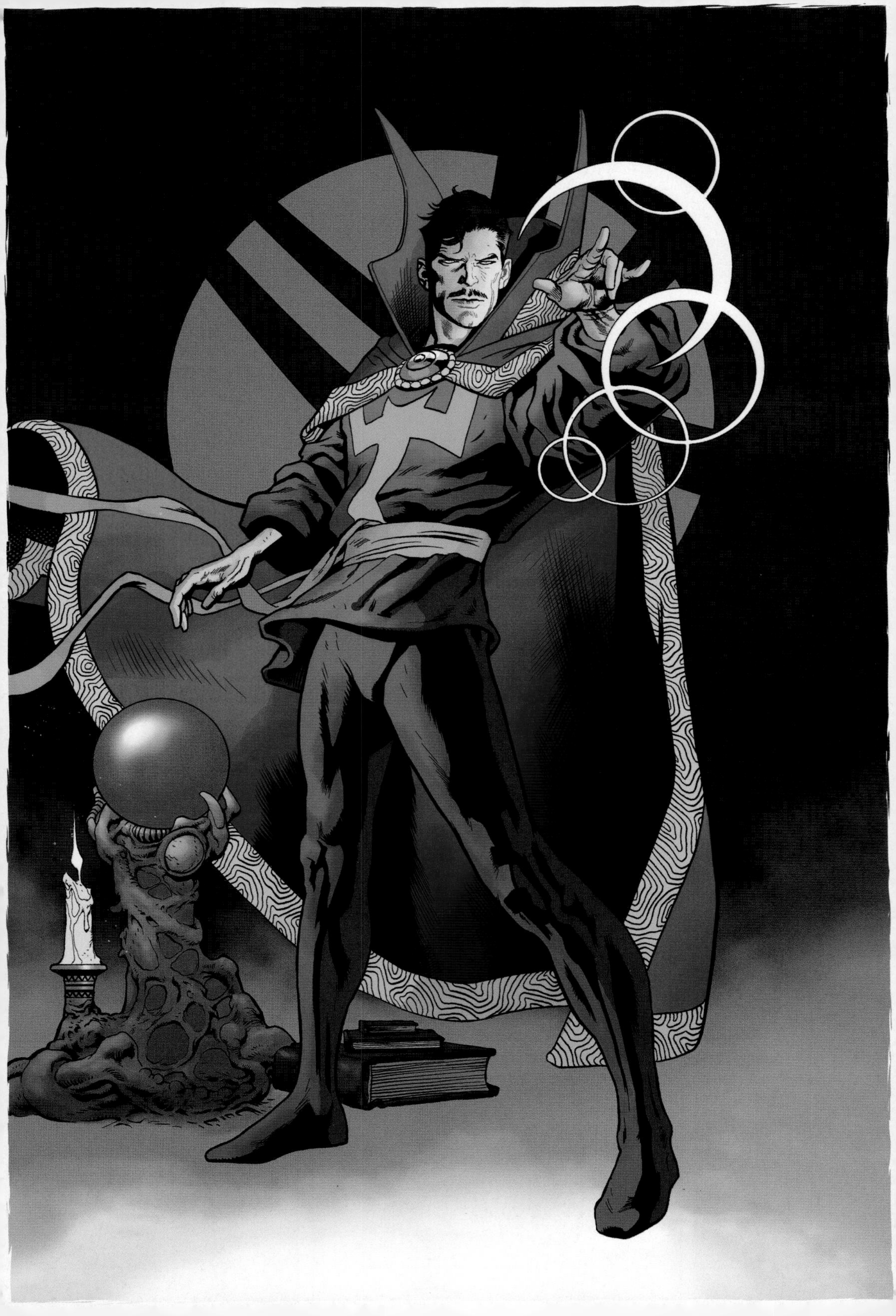

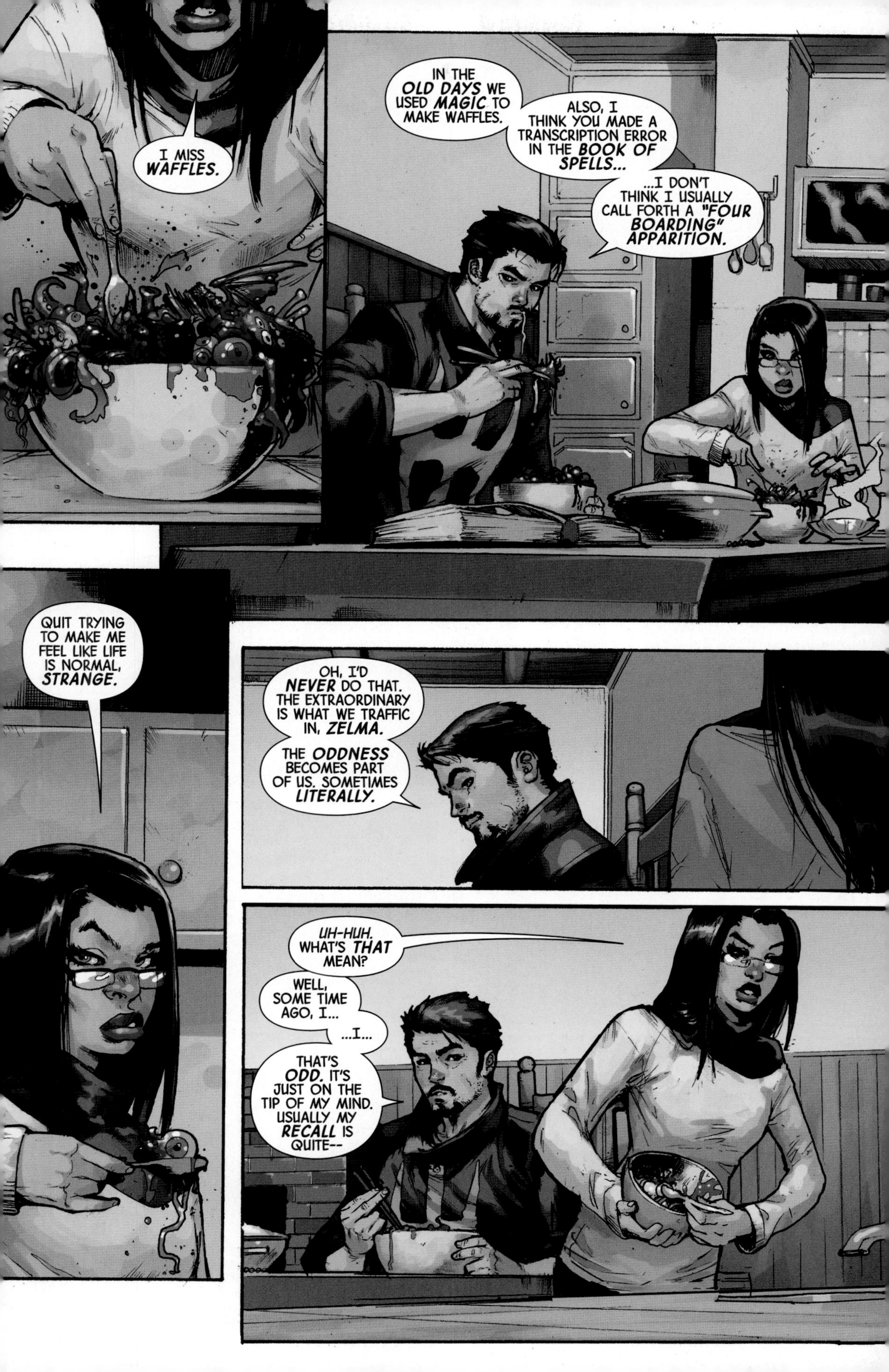
I MISS WAFFLES.
IN THE OLD DAYS WE USED MAGIC TO MAKE WAFFLES.
ALSO, I THINK YOU MADE A TRANSCRIPTION ERROR IN THE BOOK OF SPELLS...
...I DON'T THINK I USUALLY CALL FORTH A "FOUR BOARDING" APPARITION.
QUIT TRYING TO MAKE ME FEEL LIKE LIFE IS NORMAL, STRANGE.
OH, I'D NEVER DO THAT. THE EXTRAORDINARY IS WHAT WE TRAFFIC IN, ZELMA.
THE ODDNESS BECOMES PART OF US. SOMETIMES LITERALLY.
UH-HUH. WHAT'S THAT MEAN?
WELL, SOME TIME AGO, I...
...I...
THAT'S ODD. IT'S JUST ON THE TIP OF MY MIND. USUALLY MY RECALL IS QUITE--

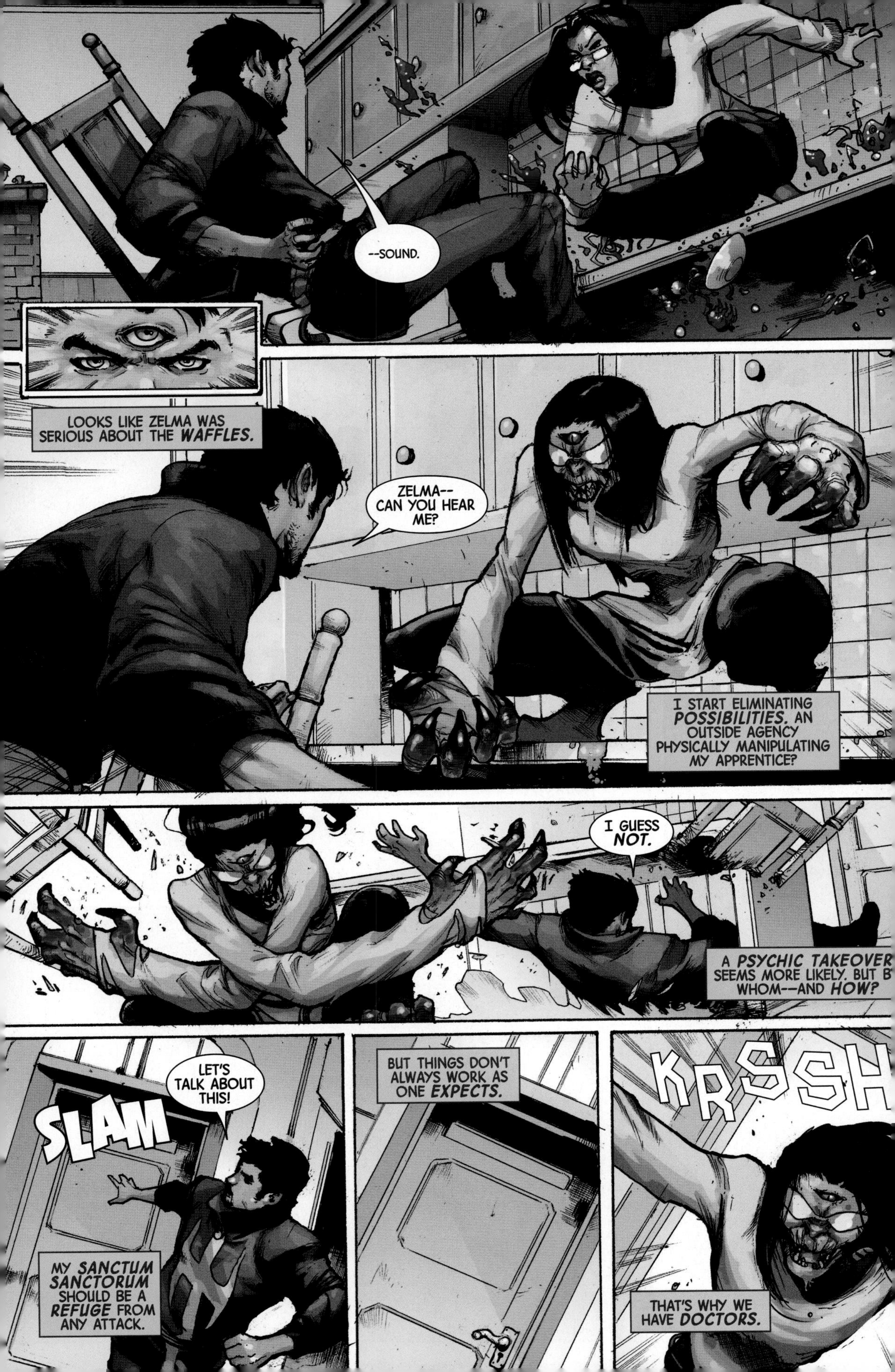
--SOUND.
LOOKS LIKE ZELMA WAS SERIOUS ABOUT THE WAFFLES.
ZELMA-- CAN YOU HEAR ME?
I START ELIMINATING POSSIBILITIES. AN OUTSIDE AGENCY PHYSICALLY MANIPULATING MY APPRENTICE?
I GUESS NOT.
A PSYCHIC TAKEOVER SEEMS MORE LIKELY. BUT B WHOM--AND HOW?
LET'S TALK ABOUT THIS!
SLAM
MY SANCTUM SANCTORUM SHOULD BE A REFUGE FROM ANY ATTACK.
BUT THINGS DON'T ALWAYS WORK AS ONE EXPECTS.
KRSSH
THAT'S WHY WE HAVE DOCTORS.

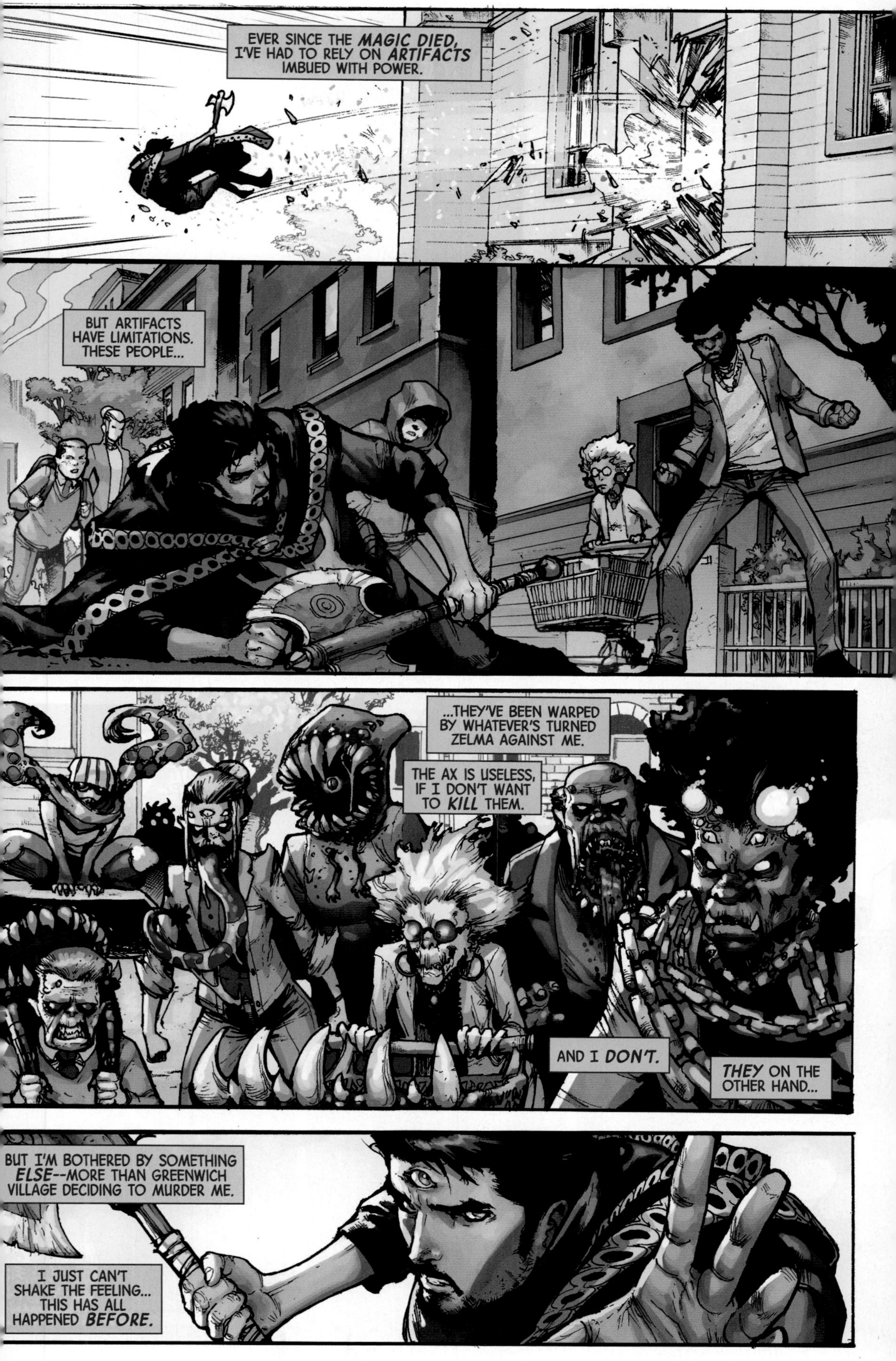
EVER SINCE THE MAGIC DIED, I'VE HAD TO RELY ON ARTIFACTS IMBUED WITH POWER.
BUT ARTIFACTS HAVE LIMITATIONS. THESE PEOPLE...
...THEY'VE BEEN WARPED BY WHATEVER'S TURNED ZELMA AGAINST ME.
THE AX IS USELESS, IF I DON'T WANT TO KILL THEM.
AND I DON'T.
THEY ON THE OTHER HAND...
BUT I'M BOTHERED BY SOMETHING ELSE--MORE THAN GREENWICH VILLAGE DECIDING TO MURDER ME.
I JUST CAN'T SHAKE THE FEELING... THIS HAS ALL HAPPENED BEFORE.

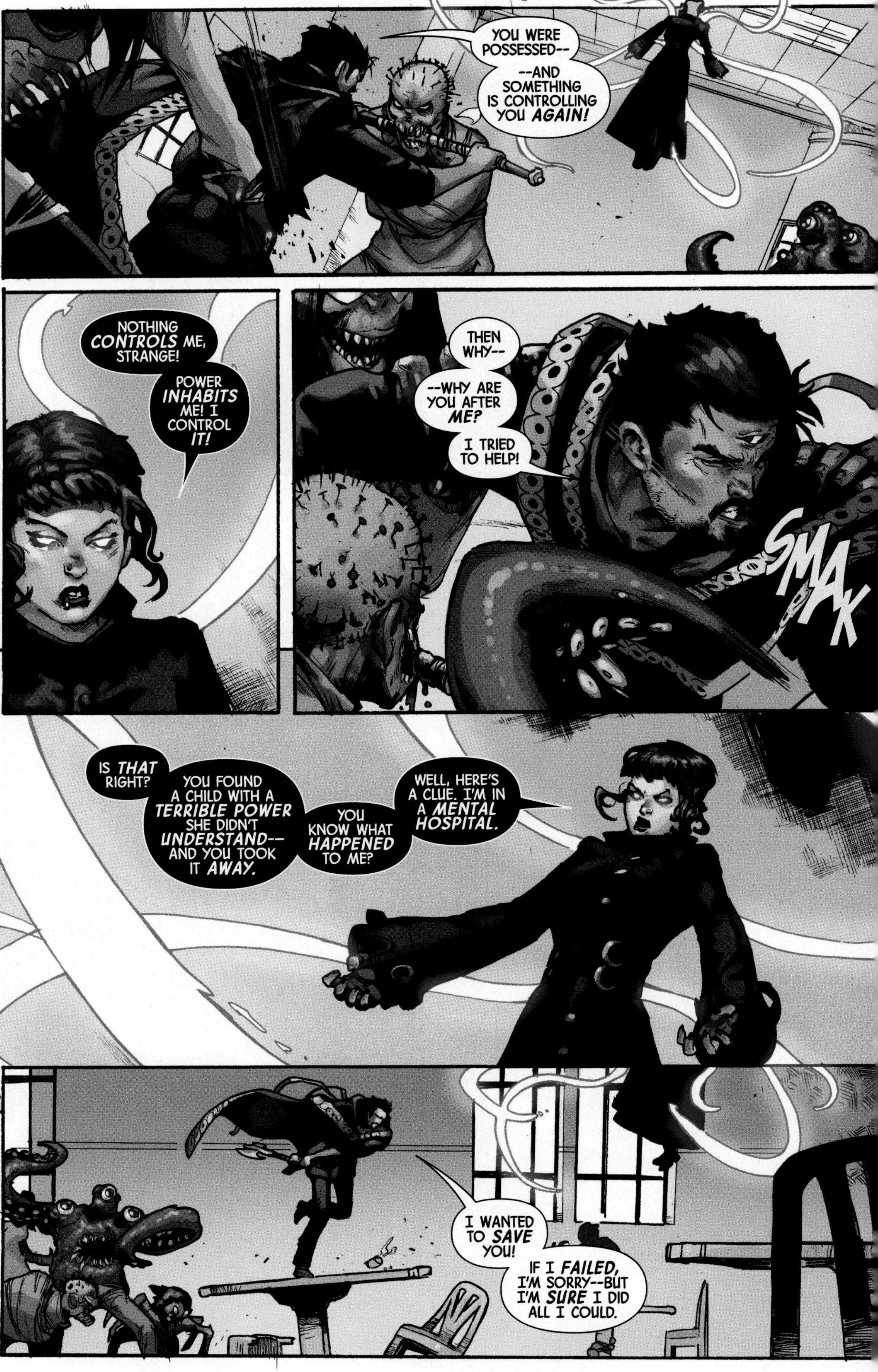

YOU WERE POSSESSED--
--AND SOMETHING IS CONTROLLING YOU AGAIN!
NOTHING CONTROLS ME, STRANGE!
POWER INHABITS ME! I CONTROL IT!
THEN WHY--
--WHY ARE YOU AFTER ME?
I TRIED TO HELP!
SMAK
IS THAT RIGHT?
YOU FOUND A CHILD WITH A TERRIBLE POWER SHE DIDN'T UNDERSTAND-- AND YOU TOOK IT AWAY.
YOU KNOW WHAT HAPPENED TO ME?
WELL, HERE'S A CLUE. I'M IN A MENTAL HOSPITAL.
I WANTED TO SAVE YOU!
IF I FAILED, I'M SORRY--BUT I'M SURE I DID ALL I COULD.

HOW--HOW DID I GET *HERE?*

WHAT MANNER OF *ENCHANTMENT*...

...WELL... PERHAPS...

...PERHAPS IT WAS *NOTHING.*

STEPHEN--WHAT'S *HAPPENED?*

I DO NOT RECALL LEAVING *HOME*...

THE ANSWER ELUDES *ME* AS WELL, MY FRIENDS...

...YET I FEEL A WELCOME JOY IN *SEEING* YOU AGAIN.

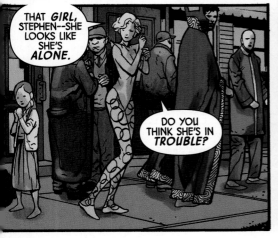

THAT *GIRL*, STEPHEN--SHE LOOKS LIKE SHE'S *ALONE.*

DO YOU THINK SHE'S IN *TROUBLE?*

SOMETIMES WE MUST *TRUST* OUR *SENSES*, CLEA--AND MY SENSES TELL ME THAT, FOR THE *MOMENT* AT LEAST...

...ALL IS *WELL* WITH THE *WORLD!*

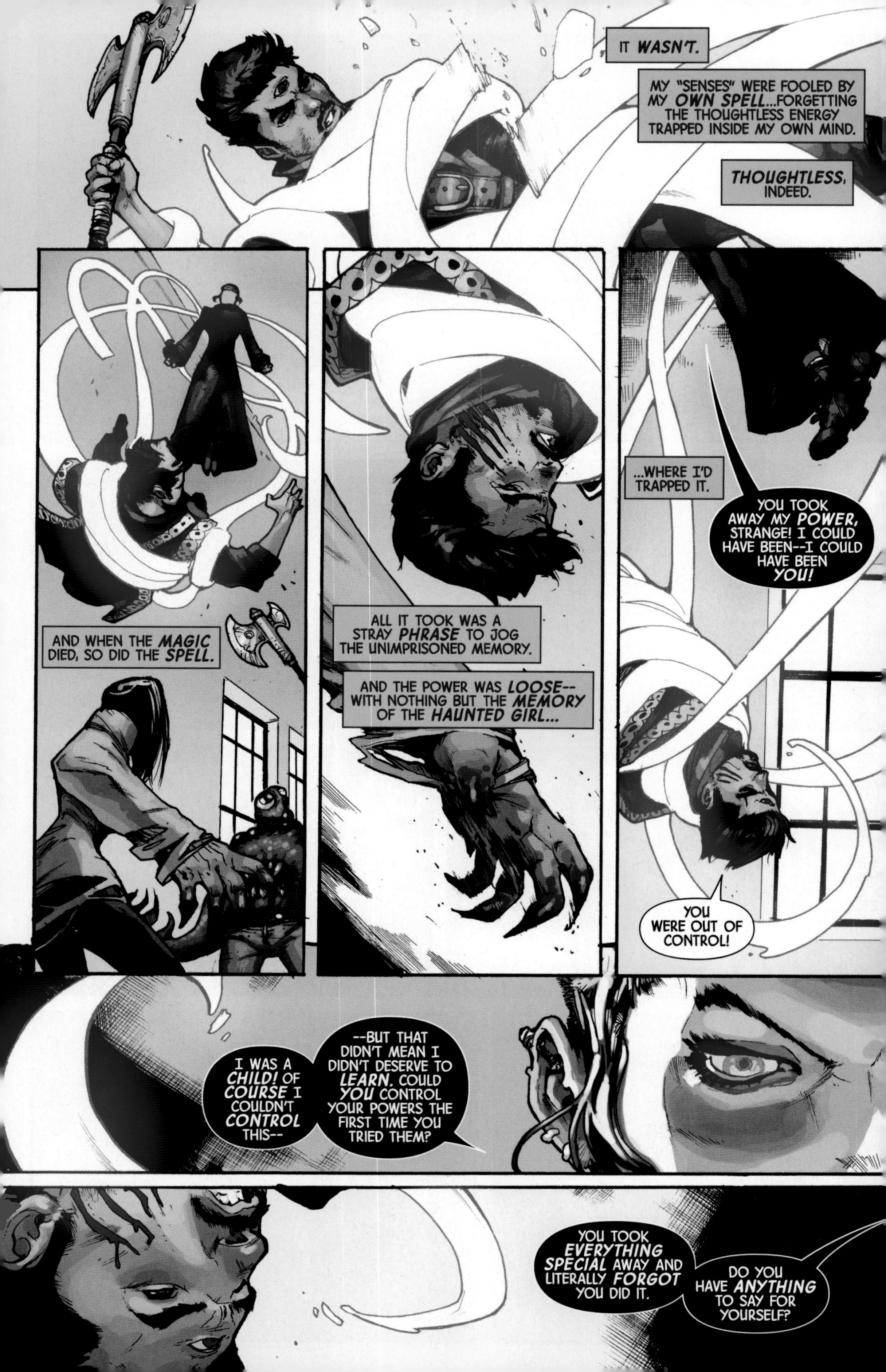

IT WASN'T.
MY "SENSES" WERE FOOLED BY MY OWN SPELL...FORGETTING THE THOUGHTLESS ENERGY TRAPPED INSIDE MY OWN MIND.
THOUGHTLESS, INDEED.
AND WHEN THE MAGIC DIED, SO DID THE SPELL.
ALL IT TOOK WAS A STRAY PHRASE TO JOG THE UNIMPRISONED MEMORY.
AND THE POWER WAS LOOSE-- WITH NOTHING BUT THE MEMORY OF THE HAUNTED GIRL...
...WHERE I'D TRAPPED IT.
YOU TOOK AWAY MY POWER, STRANGE! I COULD HAVE BEEN--I COULD HAVE BEEN YOU!
YOU WERE OUT OF CONTROL!
I WAS A CHILD! OF COURSE I COULDN'T CONTROL THIS--
--BUT THAT DIDN'T MEAN I DIDN'T DESERVE TO LEARN. COULD YOU CONTROL YOUR POWERS THE FIRST TIME YOU TRIED THEM?
YOU TOOK EVERYTHING SPECIAL AWAY AND LITERALLY FORGOT YOU DID IT.
DO YOU HAVE ANYTHING TO SAY FOR YOURSELF?

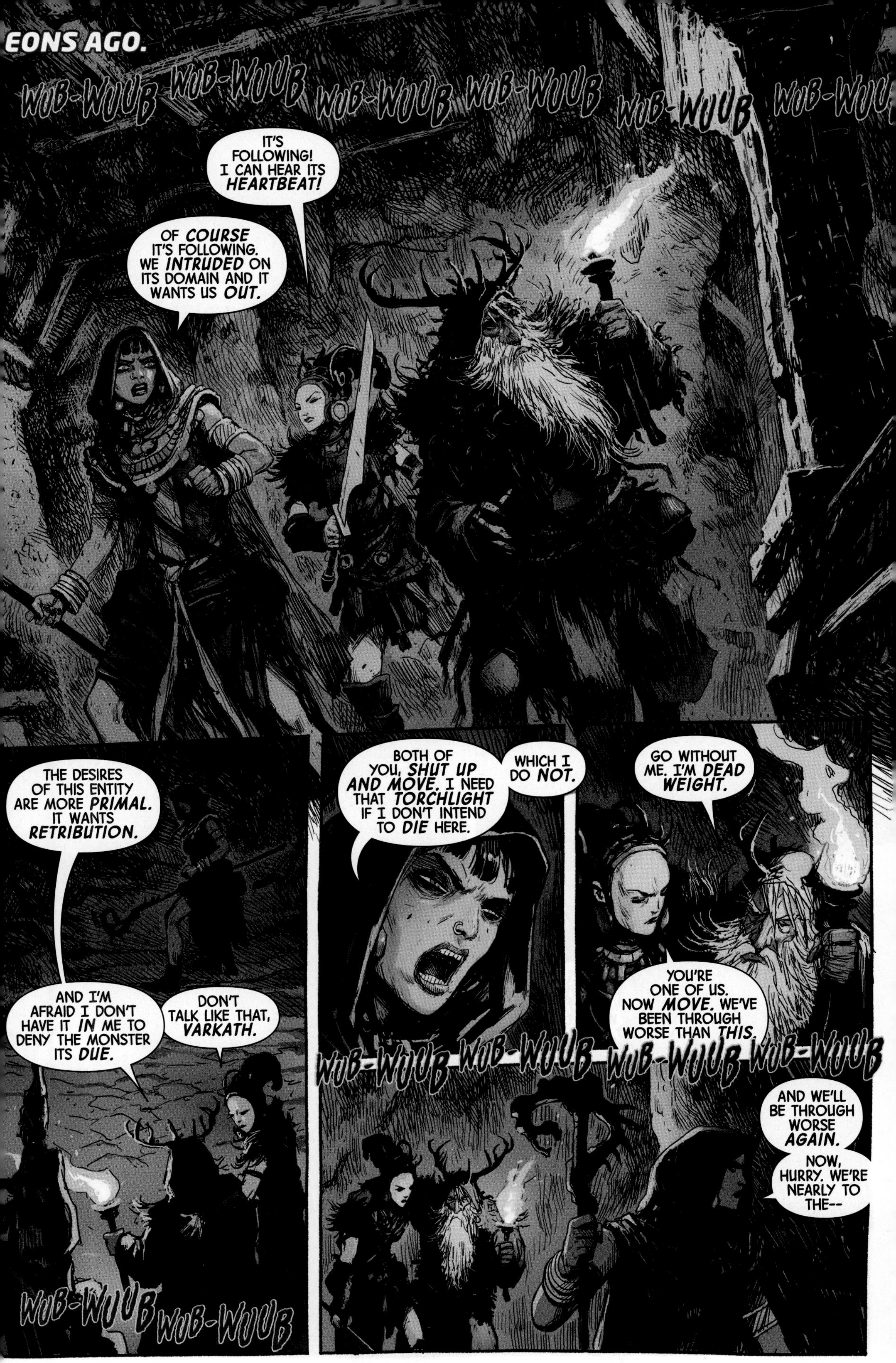
EONS AGO.
WUB-WUUB WUB-WUUB WUB-WUUB WUB-WUUB WUB-WUUB WUB-WUUB
IT'S FOLLOWING! I CAN HEAR ITS HEARTBEAT!
OF COURSE IT'S FOLLOWING. WE INTRUDED ON ITS DOMAIN AND IT WANTS US OUT.
THE DESIRES OF THIS ENTITY ARE MORE PRIMAL. IT WANTS RETRIBUTION.
AND I'M AFRAID I DON'T HAVE IT IN ME TO DENY THE MONSTER ITS DUE.
DON'T TALK LIKE THAT, VARKATH.
WUB-WUUB WUB-WUUB
BOTH OF YOU, SHUT UP AND MOVE. I NEED THAT TORCHLIGHT IF I DON'T INTEND TO DIE HERE.
WHICH I DO NOT.
GO WITHOUT ME. I'M DEAD WEIGHT.
YOU'RE ONE OF US. NOW MOVE. WE'VE BEEN THROUGH WORSE THAN THIS.
WUB-WUUB WUB-WUUB WUB-WUUB WUB-WUUB
AND WE'LL BE THROUGH WORSE AGAIN.
NOW, HURRY. WE'RE NEARLY TO THE--

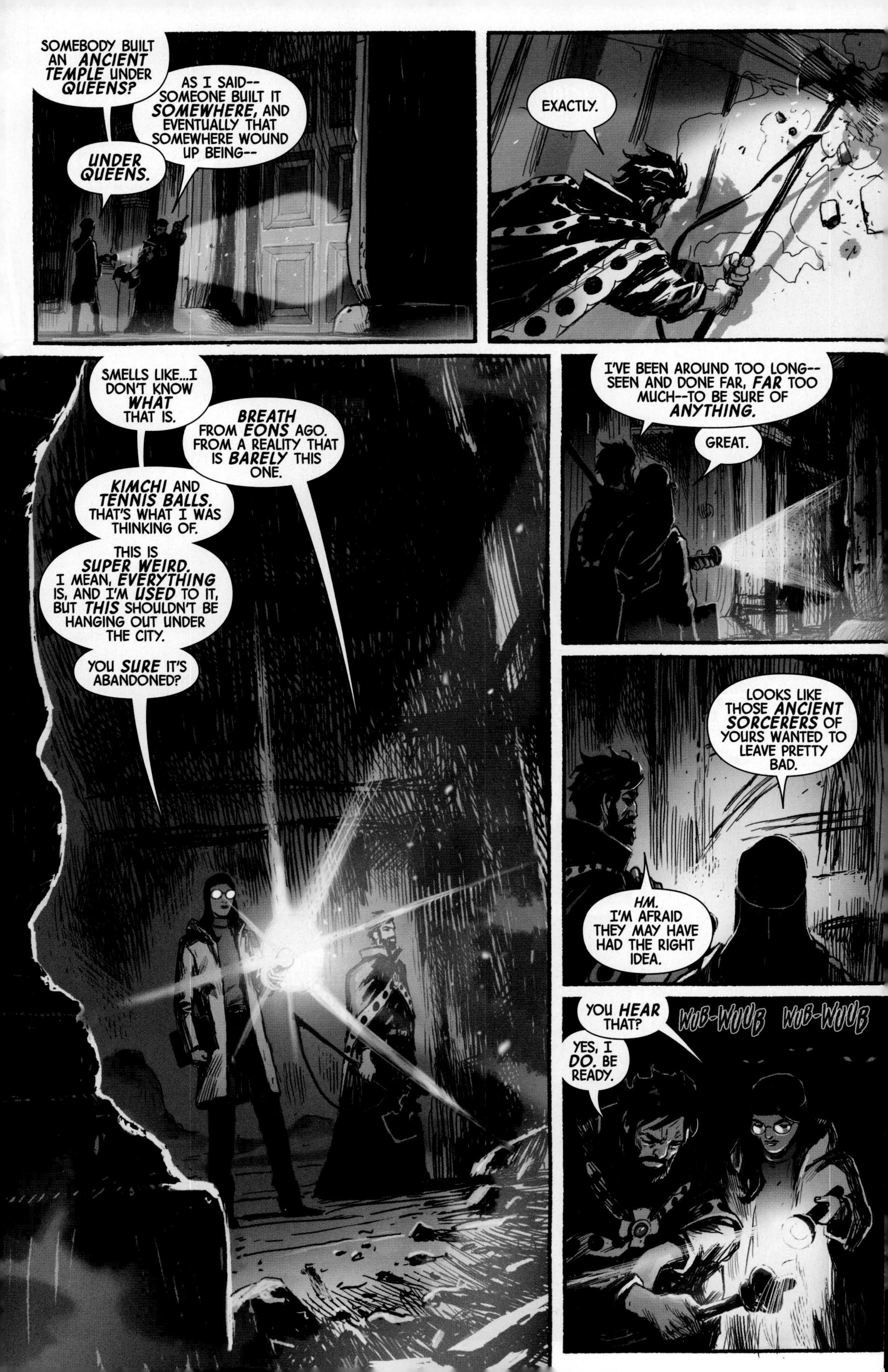
SOMEBODY BUILT AN ANCIENT TEMPLE UNDER QUEENS?
AS I SAID-- SOMEONE BUILT IT SOMEWHERE, AND EVENTUALLY THAT SOMEWHERE WOUND UP BEING--
UNDER QUEENS.
EXACTLY.
SMELLS LIKE...I DON'T KNOW WHAT THAT IS.
BREATH FROM EONS AGO. FROM A REALITY THAT IS BARELY THIS ONE.
KIMCHI AND TENNIS BALLS. THAT'S WHAT I WAS THINKING OF.
THIS IS SUPER WEIRD. I MEAN, EVERYTHING IS, AND I'M USED TO IT, BUT THIS SHOULDN'T BE HANGING OUT UNDER THE CITY.
YOU SURE IT'S ABANDONED?
I'VE BEEN AROUND TOO LONG-- SEEN AND DONE FAR, FAR TOO MUCH--TO BE SURE OF ANYTHING.
GREAT.
LOOKS LIKE THOSE ANCIENT SORCERERS OF YOURS WANTED TO LEAVE PRETTY BAD.
HM. I'M AFRAID THEY MAY HAVE HAD THE RIGHT IDEA.
YOU HEAR THAT?
WUB-WUUB WUB-WUUB
YES, I DO. BE READY.

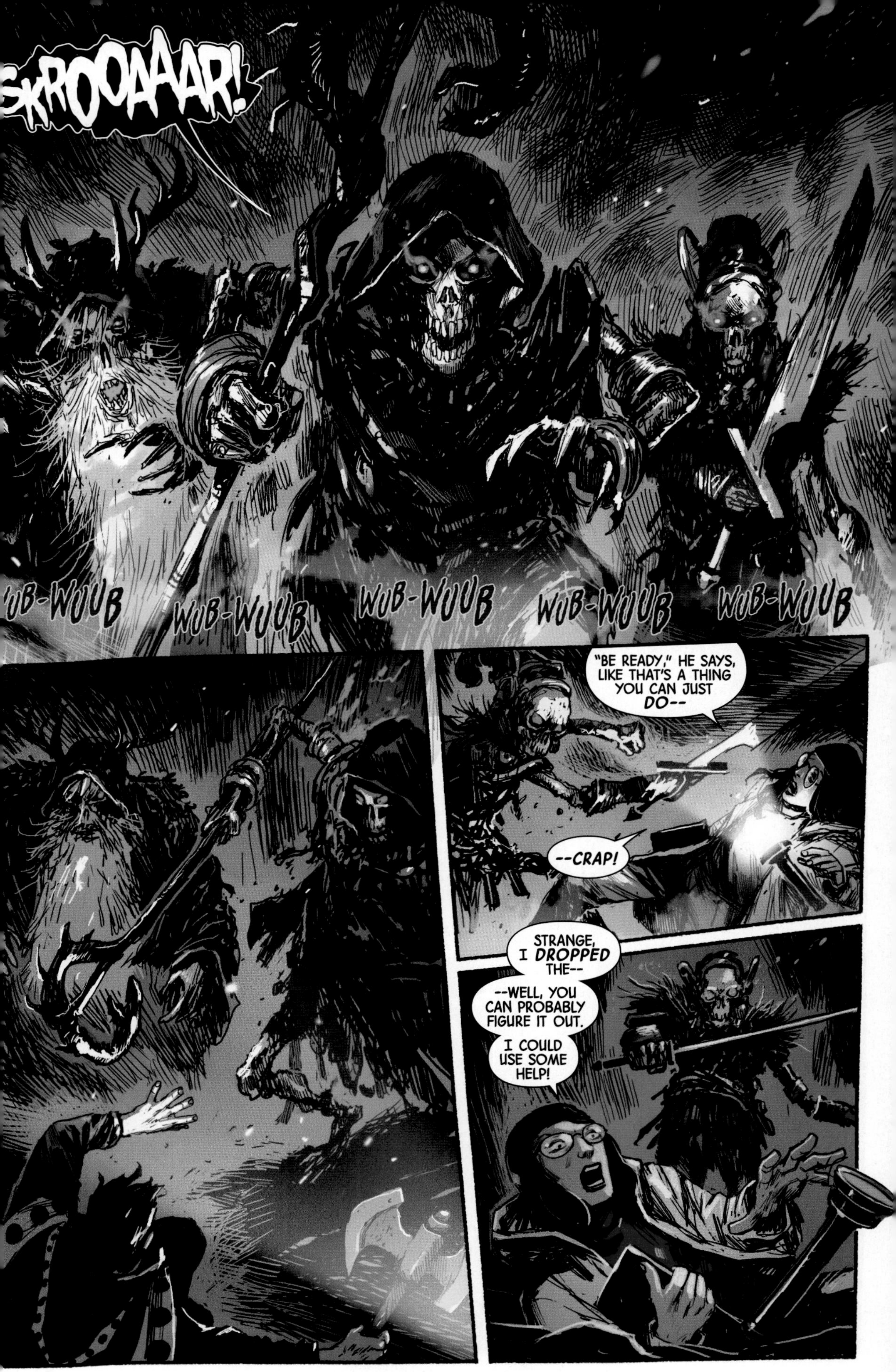
SKROOAAAR!
WUB-WUUB
WUB-WUUB
WUB-WUUB
WUB-WUUB
WUB-WUUB
"BE READY," HE SAYS, LIKE THAT'S A THING YOU CAN JUST DO--
--CRAP!
STRANGE, I DROPPED THE--
--WELL, YOU CAN PROBABLY FIGURE IT OUT.
I COULD USE SOME HELP!

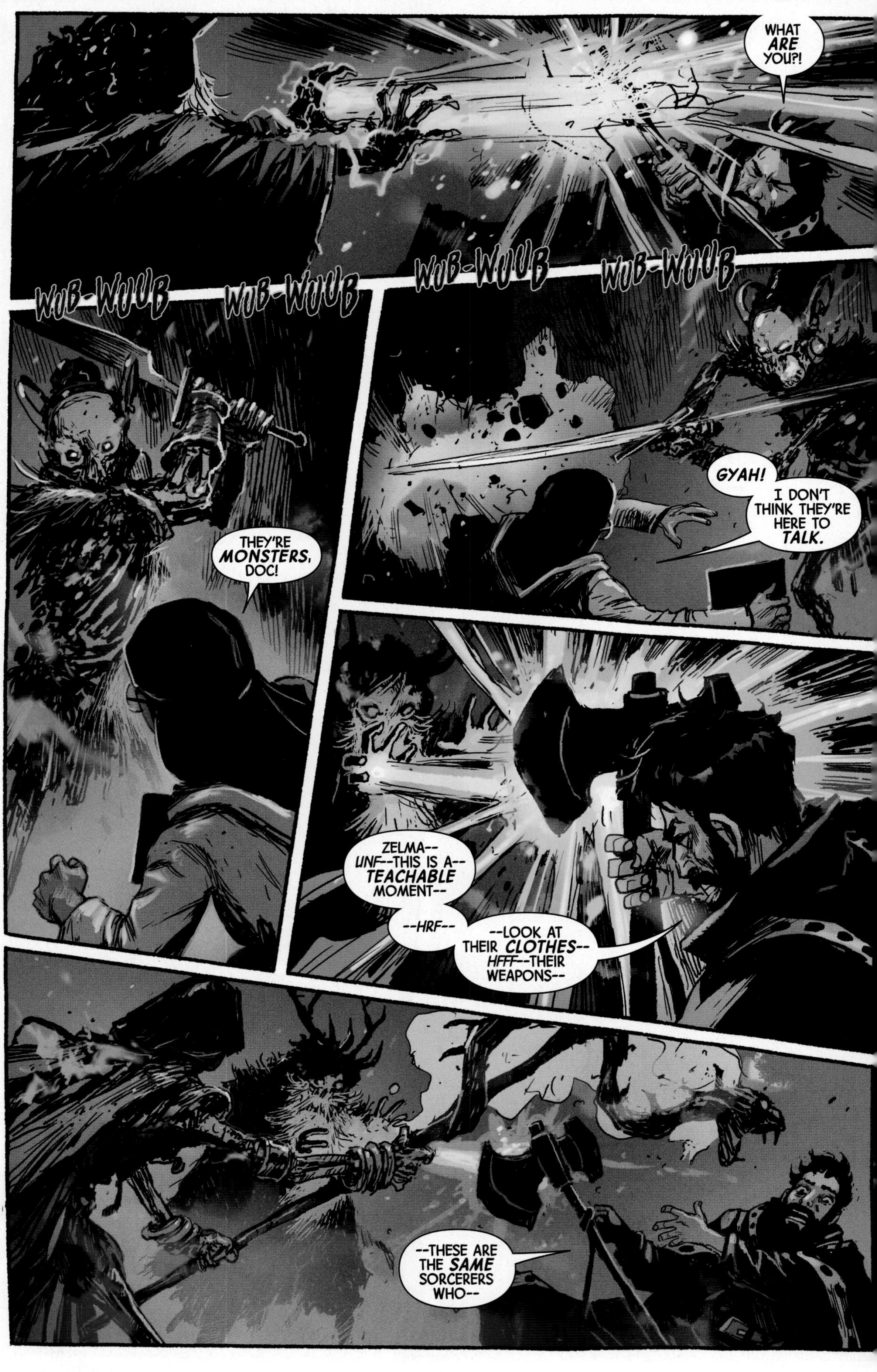
WHAT ARE YOU?!
WUB-WUUB
WUB-WUUB
WUB-WUUB
WUB-WUUB
THEY'RE MONSTERS, DOC!
GYAH!
I DON'T THINK THEY'RE HERE TO TALK.
ZELMA-- UNF--THIS IS A-- TEACHABLE MOMENT--
--HRF--
--LOOK AT THEIR CLOTHES-- HFFF--THEIR WEAPONS--
--THESE ARE THE SAME SORCERERS WHO--

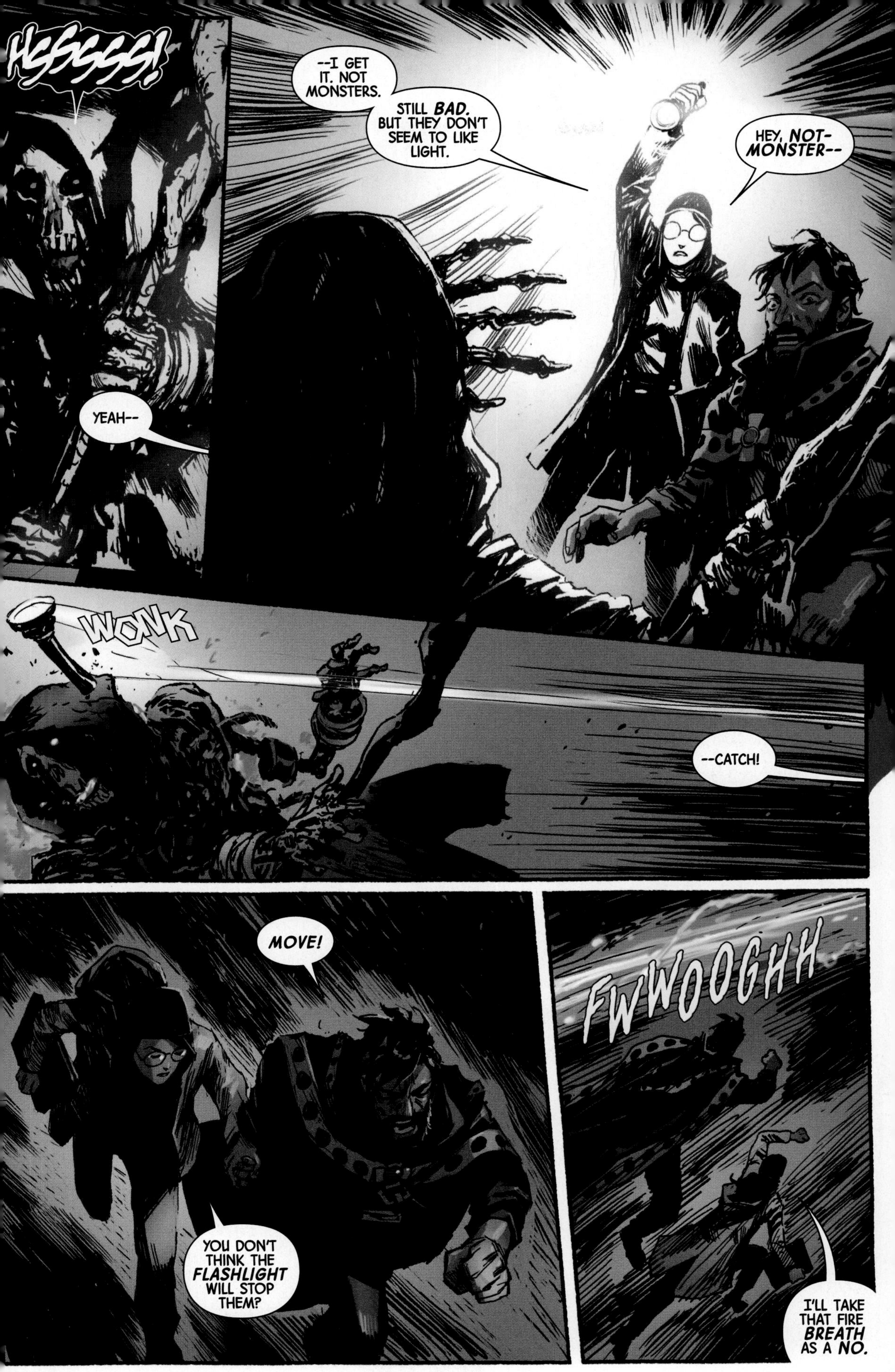
HSSSSS!
YEAH--
--I GET IT. NOT MONSTERS.
STILL *BAD.* BUT THEY DON'T SEEM TO LIKE LIGHT.
HEY, NOT-MONSTER--
WONK
--CATCH!
MOVE!
YOU DON'T THINK THE *FLASHLIGHT* WILL STOP THEM?
FWWOOGHH
I'LL TAKE THAT FIRE *BREATH* AS A *NO.*

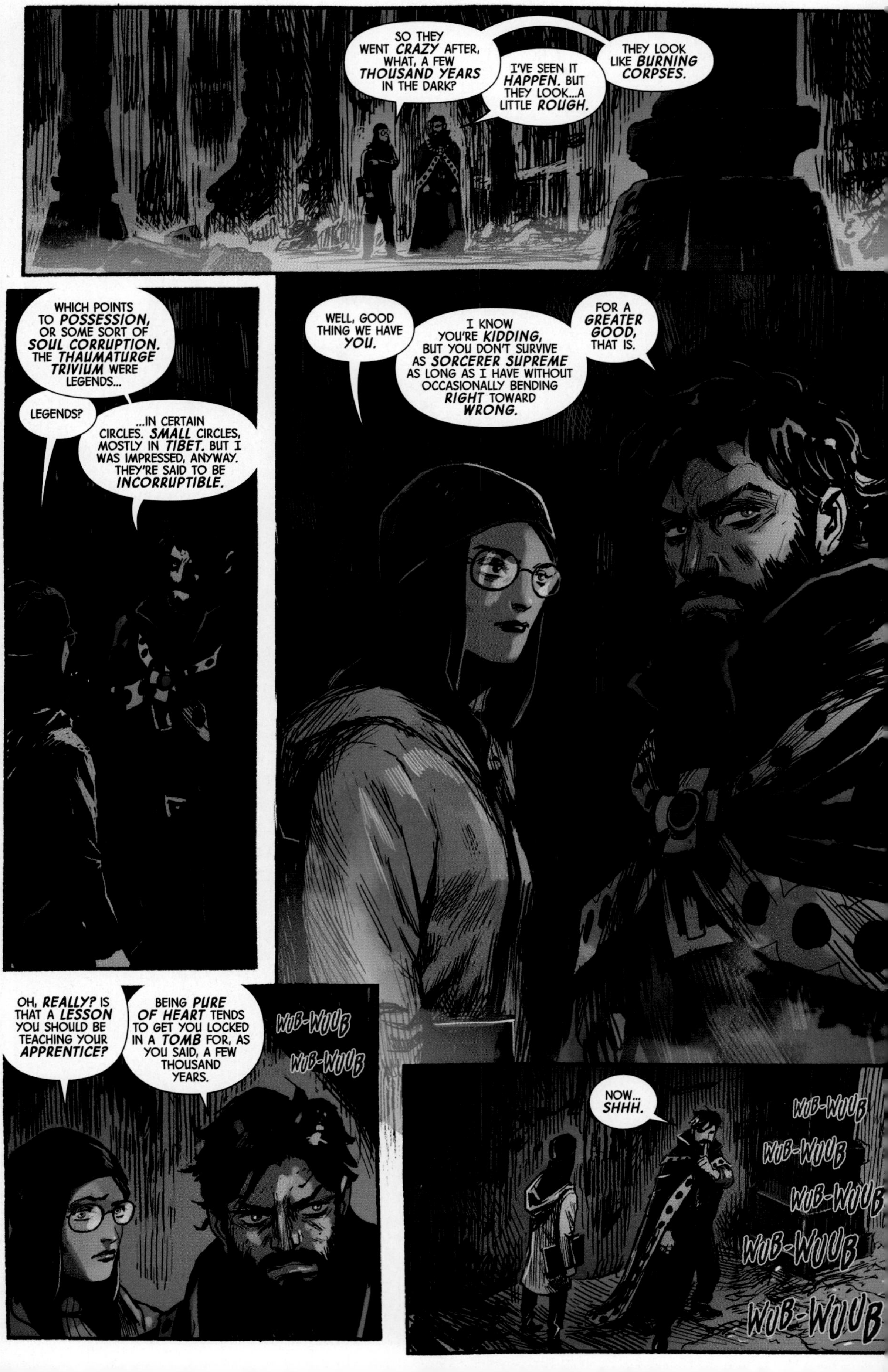
SO THEY WENT CRAZY AFTER, WHAT, A FEW THOUSAND YEARS IN THE DARK?
I'VE SEEN IT HAPPEN. BUT THEY LOOK...A LITTLE ROUGH.
THEY LOOK LIKE BURNING CORPSES.
WHICH POINTS TO POSSESSION, OR SOME SORT OF SOUL CORRUPTION. THE THAUMATURGE TRIVIUM WERE LEGENDS...
LEGENDS?
...IN CERTAIN CIRCLES. SMALL CIRCLES, MOSTLY IN TIBET. BUT I WAS IMPRESSED, ANYWAY. THEY'RE SAID TO BE INCORRUPTIBLE.
WELL, GOOD THING WE HAVE YOU.
I KNOW YOU'RE KIDDING, BUT YOU DON'T SURVIVE AS SORCERER SUPREME AS LONG AS I HAVE WITHOUT OCCASIONALLY BENDING RIGHT TOWARD WRONG.
FOR A GREATER GOOD, THAT IS.
OH, REALLY? IS THAT A LESSON YOU SHOULD BE TEACHING YOUR APPRENTICE?
BEING PURE OF HEART TENDS TO GET YOU LOCKED IN A TOMB FOR, AS YOU SAID, A FEW THOUSAND YEARS.
WUB-WUUB
WUB-WUUB
NOW... SHHH.
WUB-WUUB
WUB-WUUB
WUB-WUUB
WUB-WUUB
WUB-WUUB

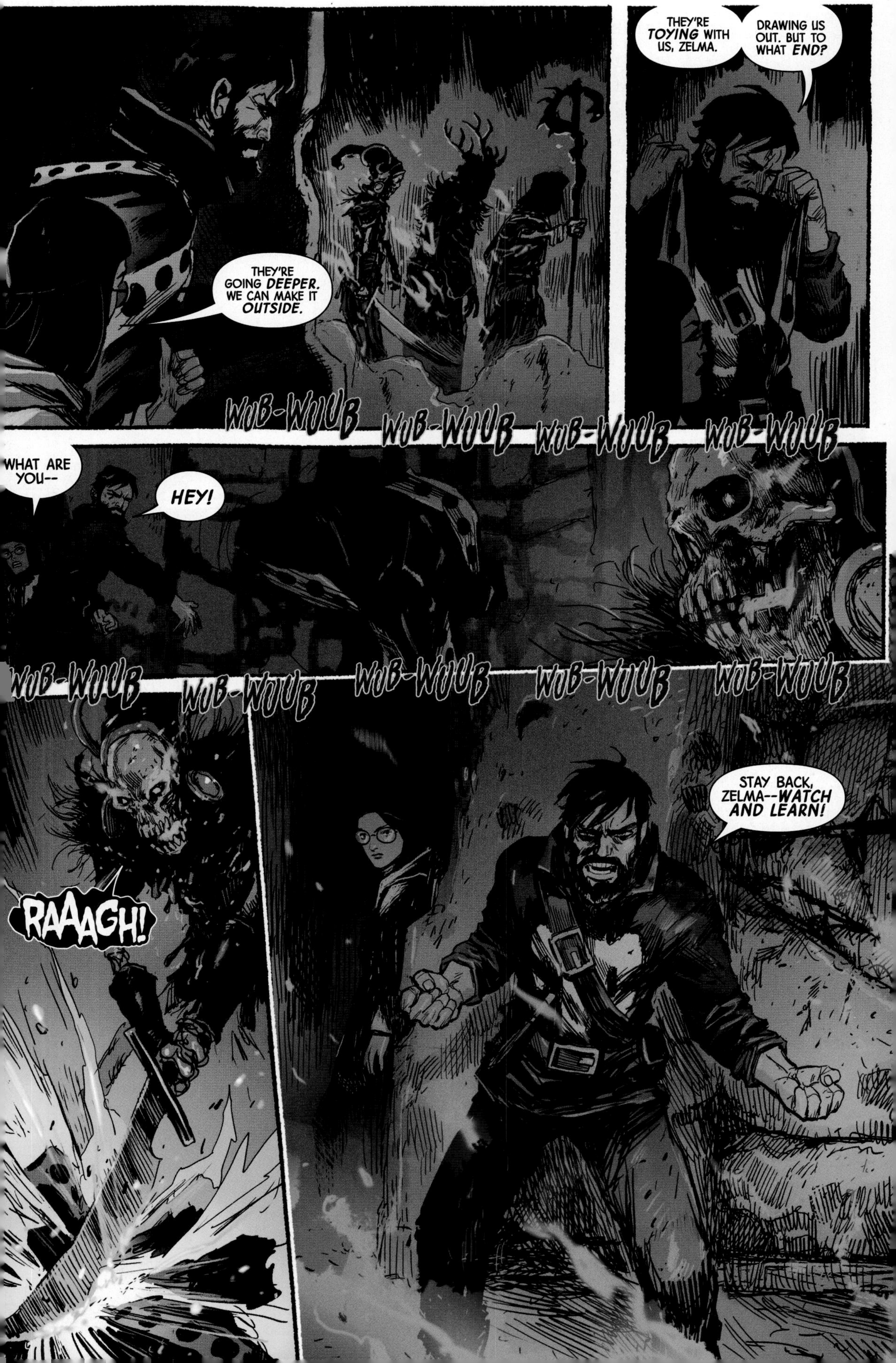

THEY'RE GOING DEEPER. WE CAN MAKE IT OUTSIDE.
THEY'RE TOYING WITH US, ZELMA.
DRAWING US OUT. BUT TO WHAT END?
WUB-WUUB WUB-WUUB WUB-WUUB WUB-WUUB
WHAT ARE YOU--
HEY!
WUB-WUUB WUB-WUUB WUB-WUUB WUB-WUUB WUB-WUUB
RAAAGH!
STAY BACK, ZELMA--WATCH AND LEARN!

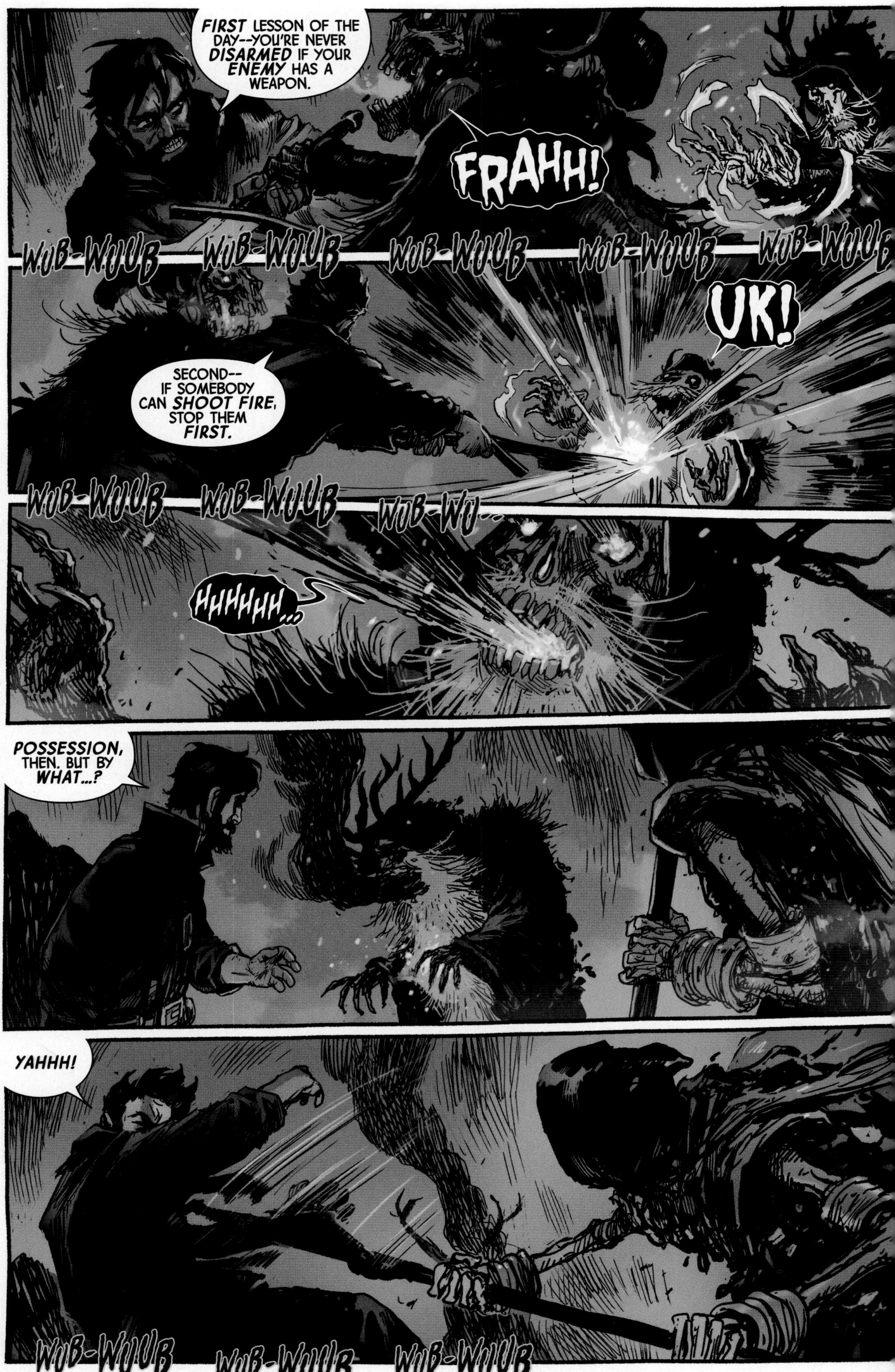
FIRST LESSON OF THE DAY--YOU'RE NEVER DISARMED IF YOUR ENEMY HAS A WEAPON.
FRAHH!
WUB-WUUB WUB-WUUB WUB-WUUB WUB-WUUB WUB-WUUB
UK!
SECOND-- IF SOMEBODY CAN SHOOT FIRE, STOP THEM FIRST.
WUB-WUUB WUB-WUUB WUB-WU--
HHHHHH...
POSSESSION, THEN. BUT BY WHAT...?
YAHHH!
WUB-WUUB WUB-WUUB WUB-WUUB

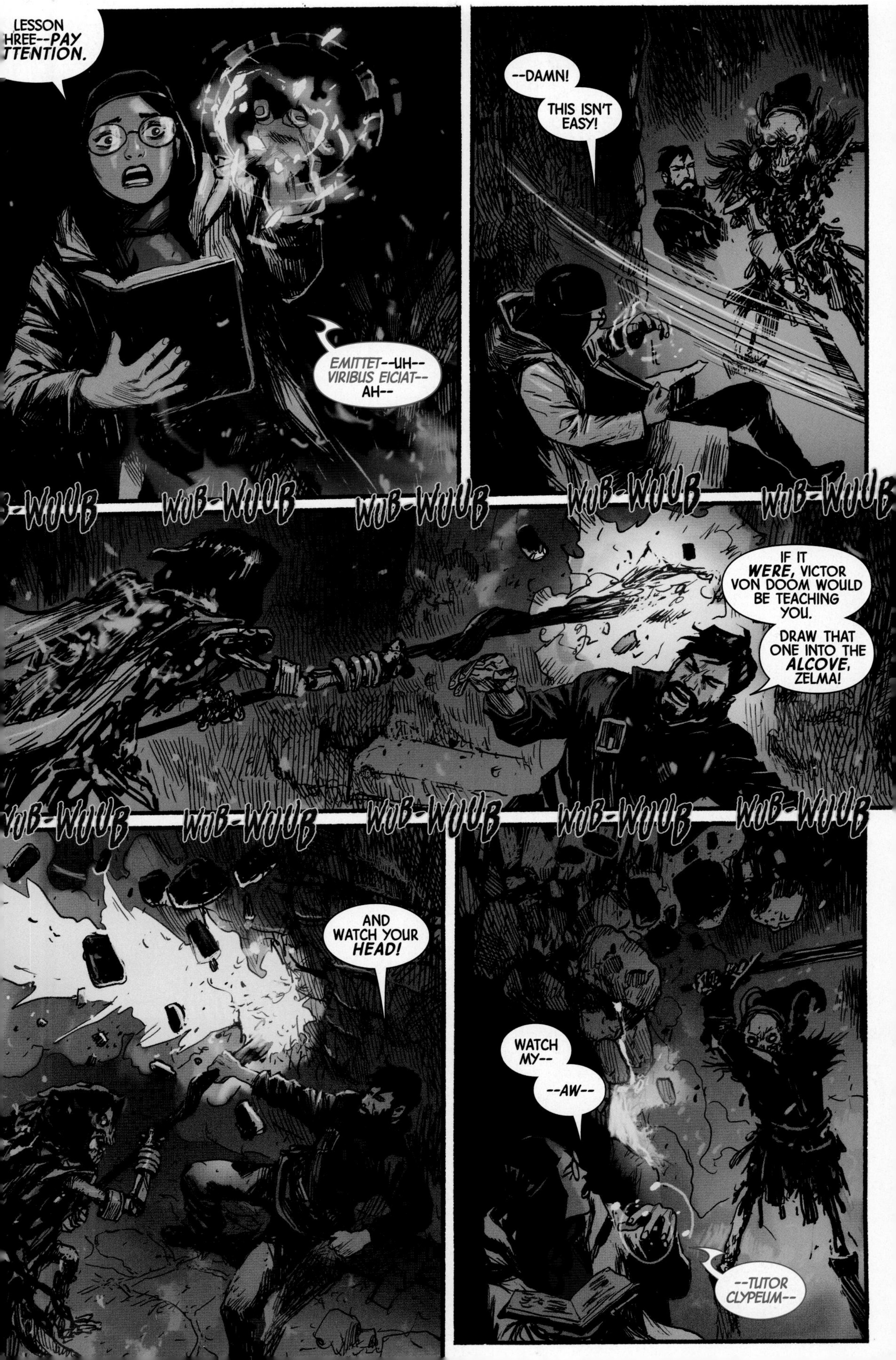
LESSON THREE--PAY ATTENTION.
EMITTET--UH--VIRIBUS EICIAT--AH--
--DAMN!
THIS ISN'T EASY!
WUB-WUUB WUB-WUUB WUB-WUUB WUB-WUUB WUB-WUUB
IF IT WERE, VICTOR VON DOOM WOULD BE TEACHING YOU.
DRAW THAT ONE INTO THE ALCOVE, ZELMA!
WUB-WUUB WUB-WUUB WUB-WUUB WUB-WUUB WUB-WUUB
AND WATCH YOUR HEAD!
WATCH MY--
--AW--
--TUTOR CLYPEUM--

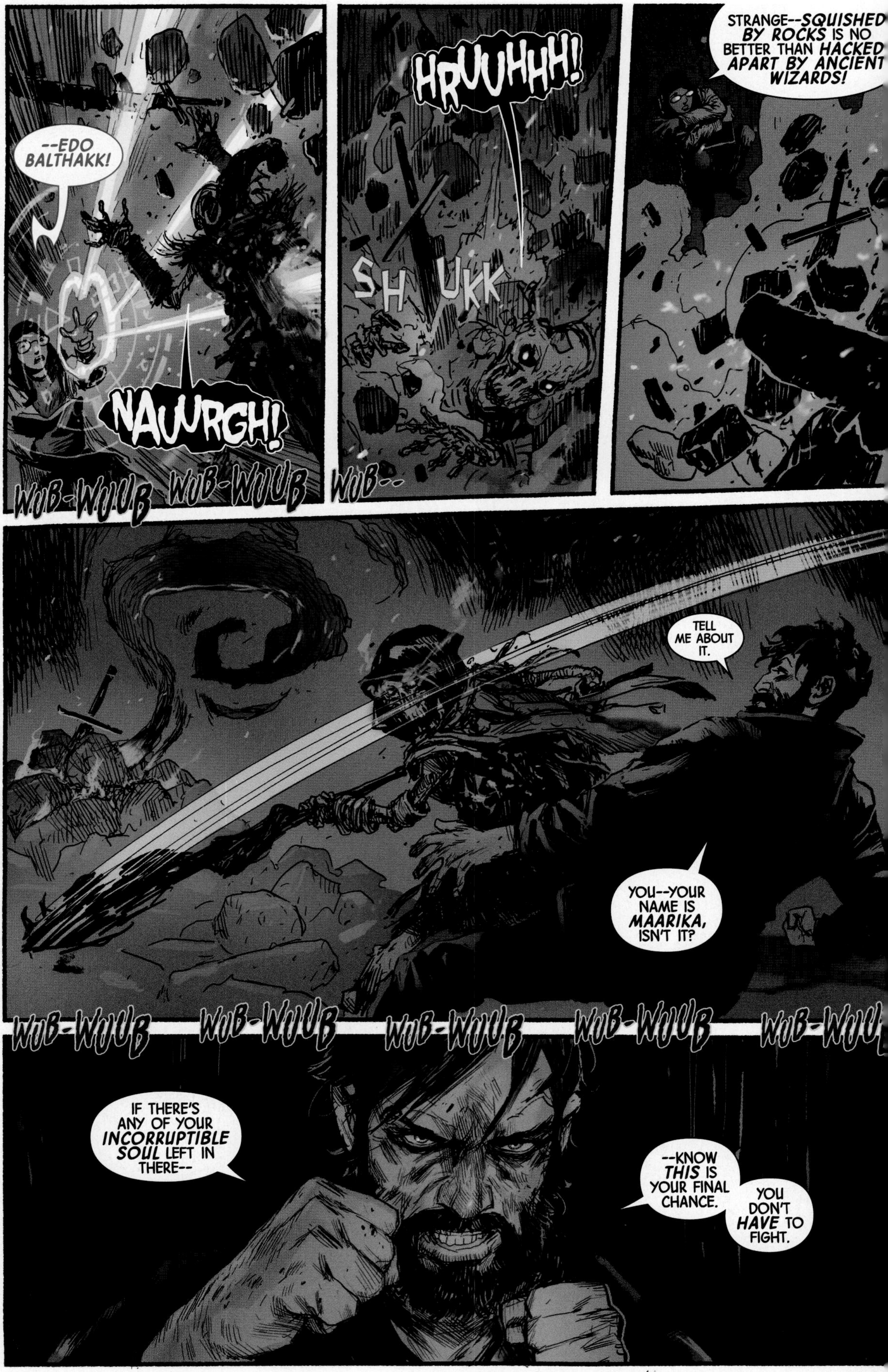
--EDO BALTHAKK!
NAUURGH!
WUB-WUUB
WUB-WUUB
HRUUHHH!
SHUKK
WUB--
STRANGE--SQUISHED BY ROCKS IS NO BETTER THAN HACKED APART BY ANCIENT WIZARDS!
TELL ME ABOUT IT.
YOU--YOUR NAME IS MAARIKA, ISN'T IT?
WUB-WUUB
WUB-WUUB
WUB-WUUB
WUB-WUUB
IF THERE'S ANY OF YOUR INCORRUPTIBLE SOUL LEFT IN THERE--
--KNOW THIS IS YOUR FINAL CHANCE.
YOU DON'T HAVE TO FIGHT.

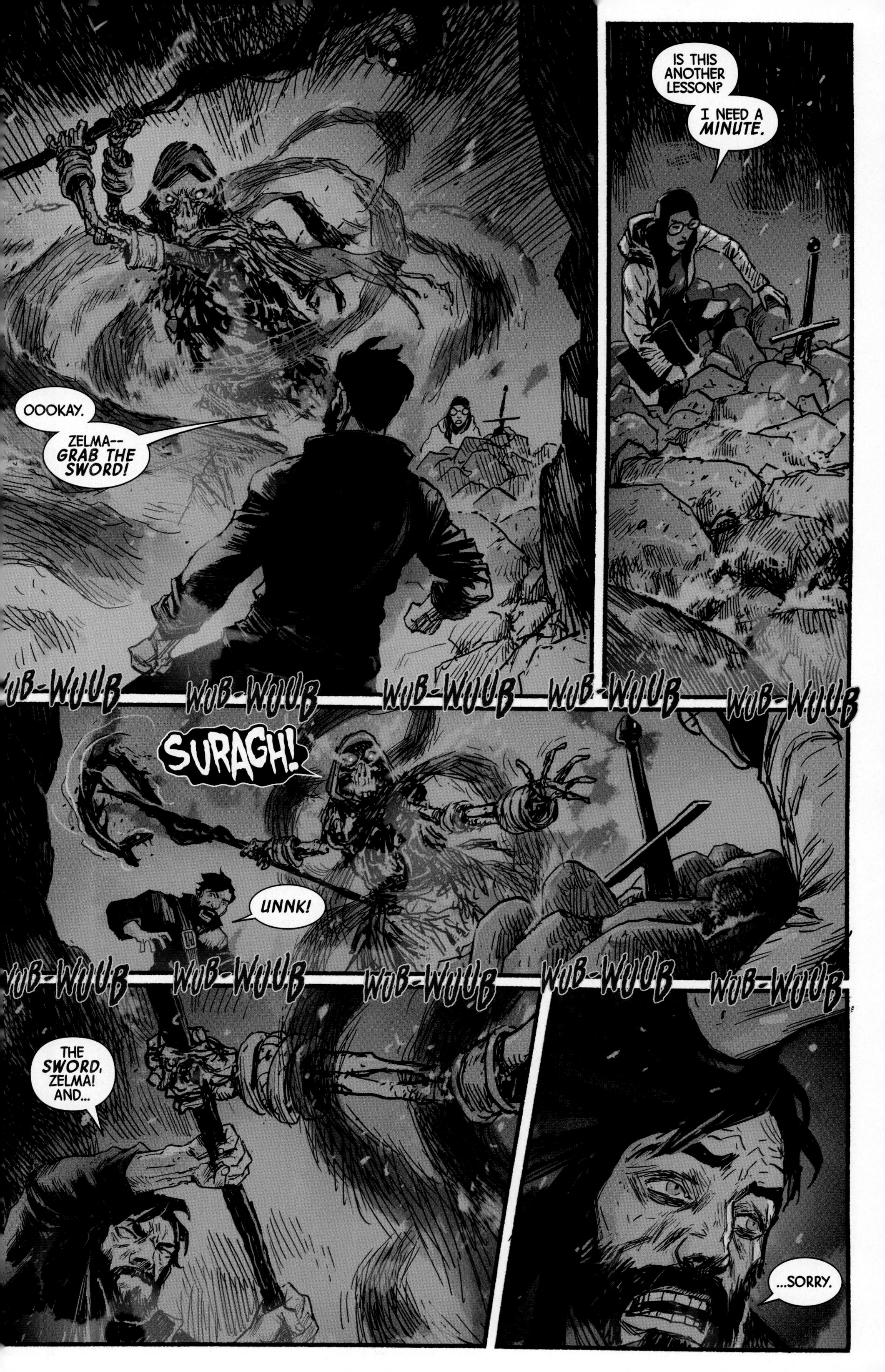
OOOKAY.
ZELMA-- GRAB THE SWORD!
IS THIS ANOTHER LESSON?
I NEED A MINUTE.
WUB-WUUB WUB-WUUB WUB-WUUB WUB-WUUB WUB-WUUB
SURAGH!
UNNK!
WUB-WUUB WUB-WUUB WUB-WUUB WUB-WUUB WUB-WUUB
THE SWORD, ZELMA! AND...
...SORRY.

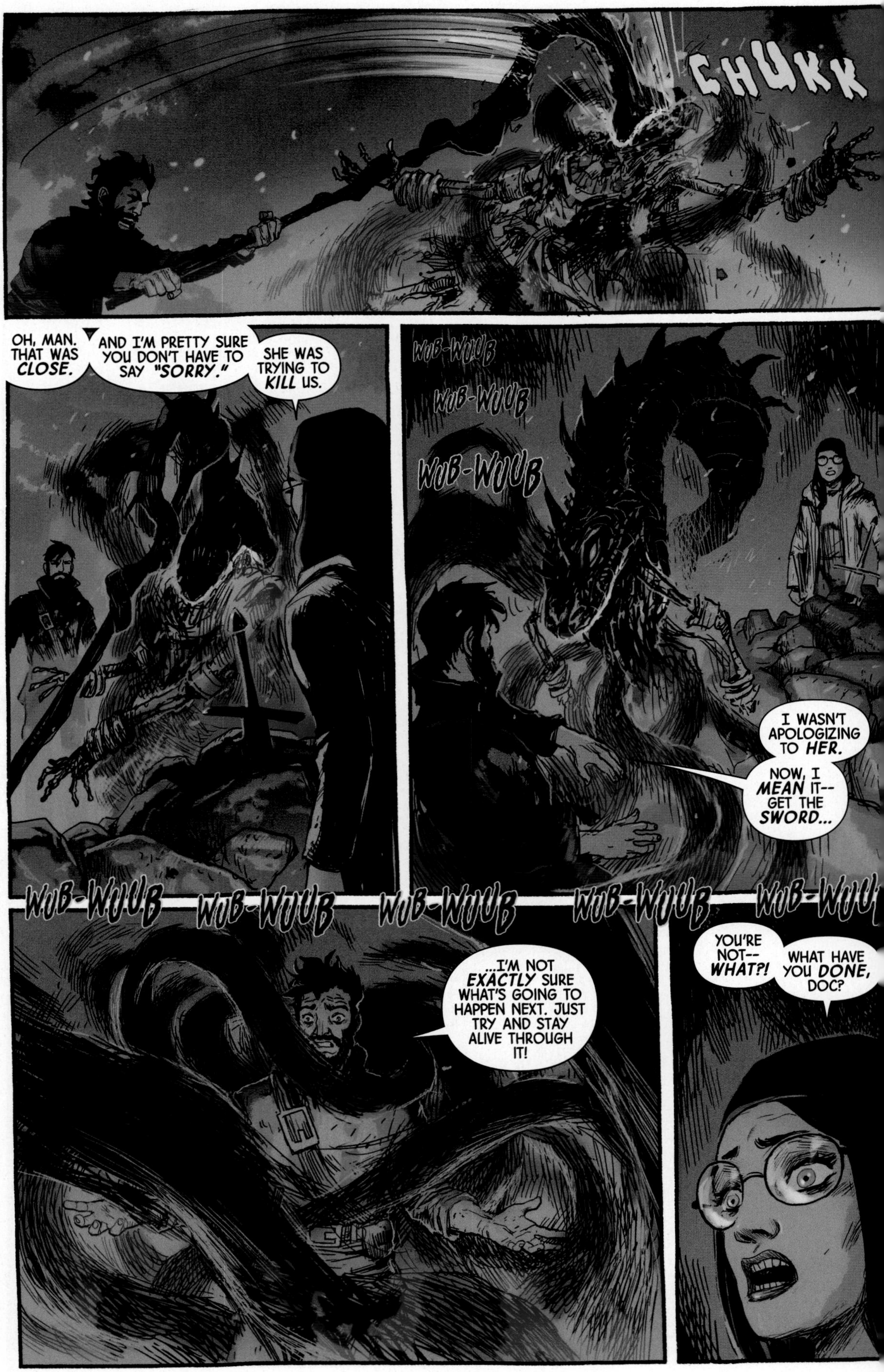
CHUKK
OH, MAN. THAT WAS CLOSE.
AND I'M PRETTY SURE YOU DON'T HAVE TO SAY "SORRY."
SHE WAS TRYING TO KILL US.
WUB-WUUB
WUB-WUUB
WUB-WUUB
I WASN'T APOLOGIZING TO HER.
NOW, I MEAN IT-- GET THE SWORD...
WUB-WUUB
WUB-WUUB
WUB-WUUB
WUB-WUUB
...I'M NOT EXACTLY SURE WHAT'S GOING TO HAPPEN NEXT. JUST TRY AND STAY ALIVE THROUGH IT!
YOU'RE NOT-- WHAT?!
WHAT HAVE YOU DONE, DOC?

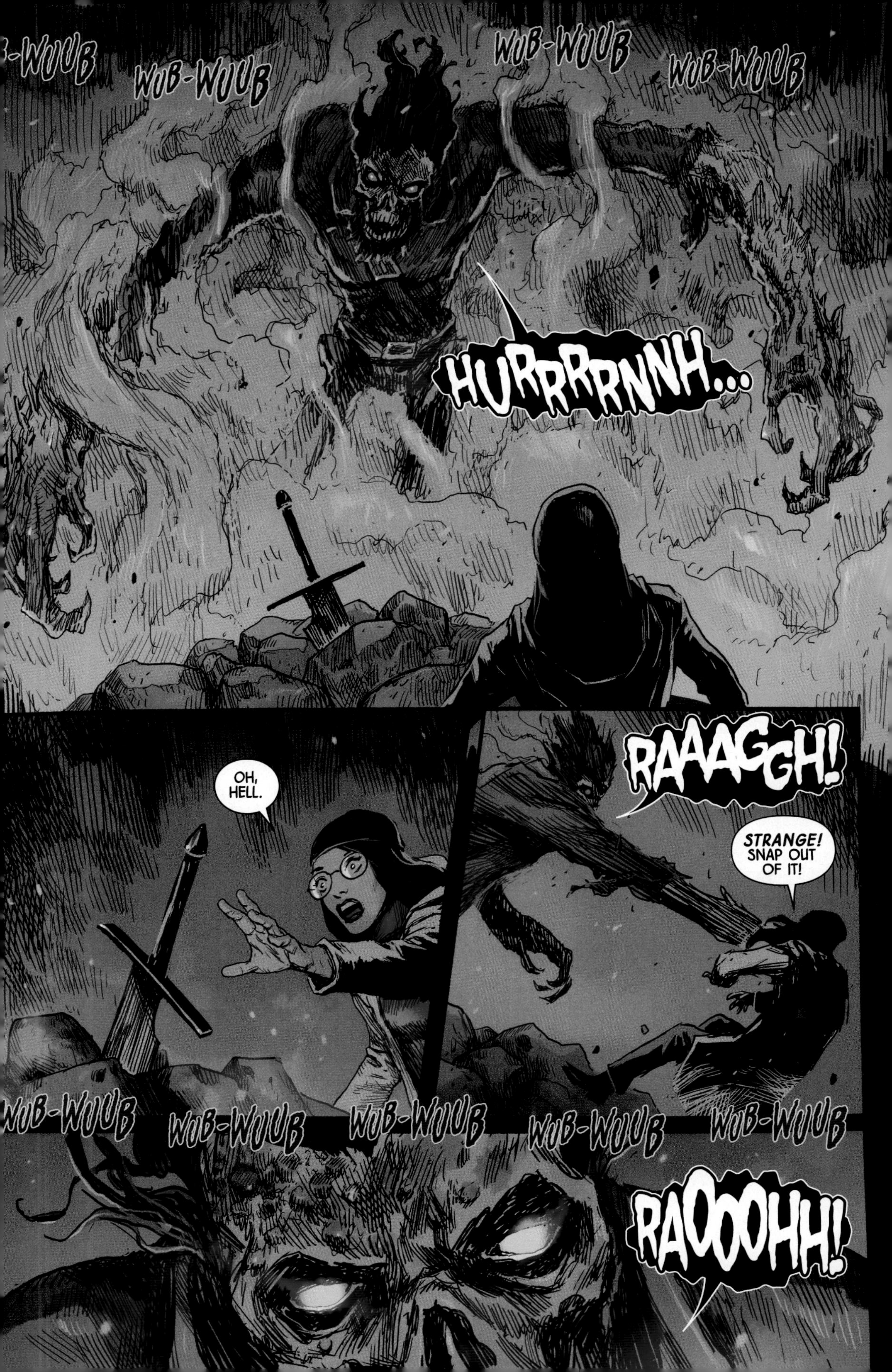
B-WUUB
WUB-WUUB
WUB-WUUB
WUB-WUUB
HURRRRNNH...
OH, HELL.
RAAAGGH!
STRANGE! SNAP OUT OF IT!
WUB-WUUB
WUB-WUUB
WUB-WUUB
WUB-WUUB
WUB-WUUB
RAOOOHH!

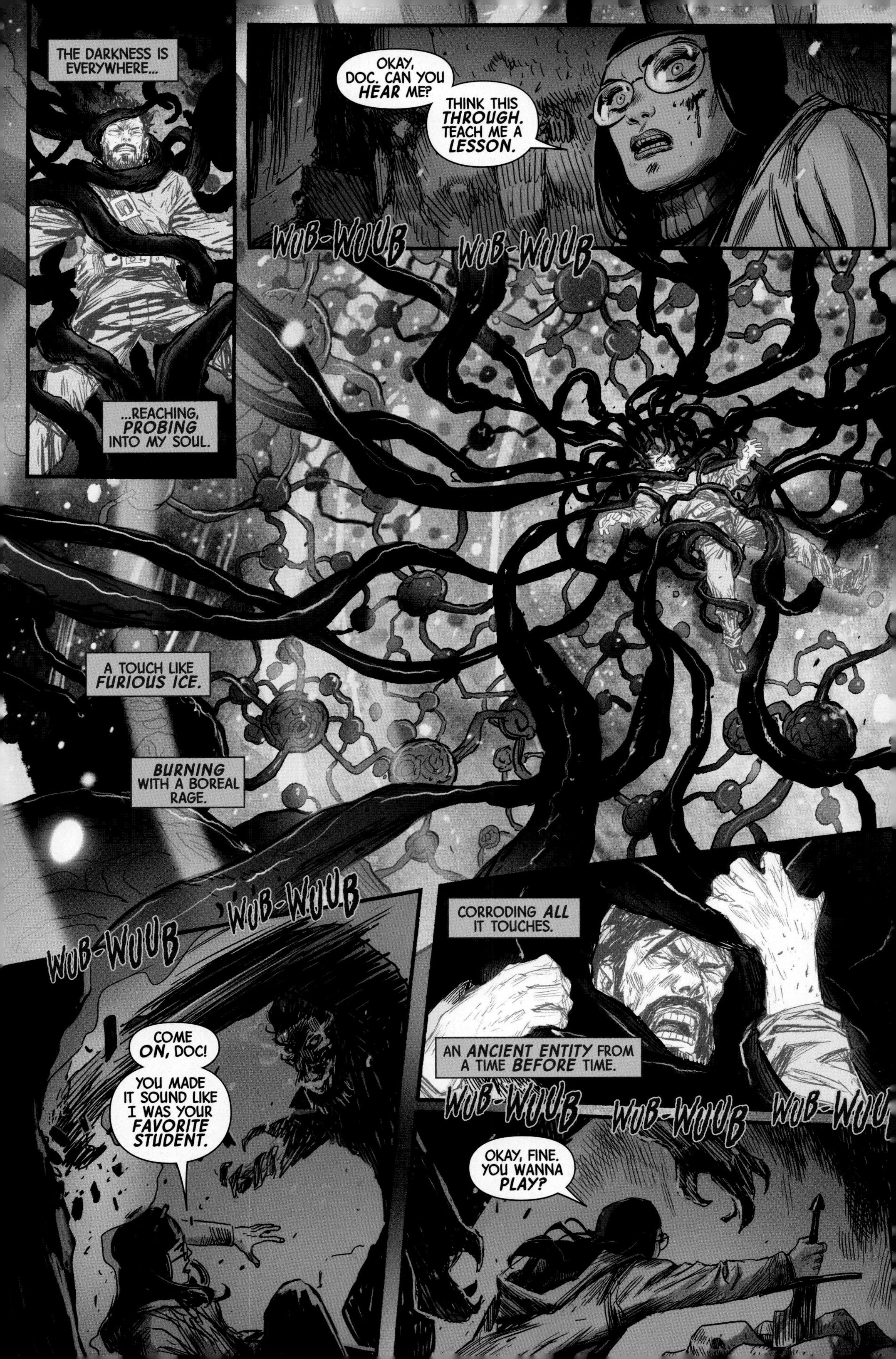
THE DARKNESS IS EVERYWHERE...
...REACHING, PROBING INTO MY SOUL.
OKAY, DOC. CAN YOU HEAR ME?
THINK THIS THROUGH. TEACH ME A LESSON.
WUB-WUUB
WUB-WUUB
A TOUCH LIKE FURIOUS ICE.
BURNING WITH A BOREAL RAGE.
WUB-WUUB
WUB-WUUB
COME ON, DOC!
YOU MADE IT SOUND LIKE I WAS YOUR FAVORITE STUDENT.
CORRODING ALL IT TOUCHES.
AN ANCIENT ENTITY FROM A TIME BEFORE TIME.
WUB-WUUB
WUB-WUUB
OKAY, FINE. YOU WANNA PLAY?

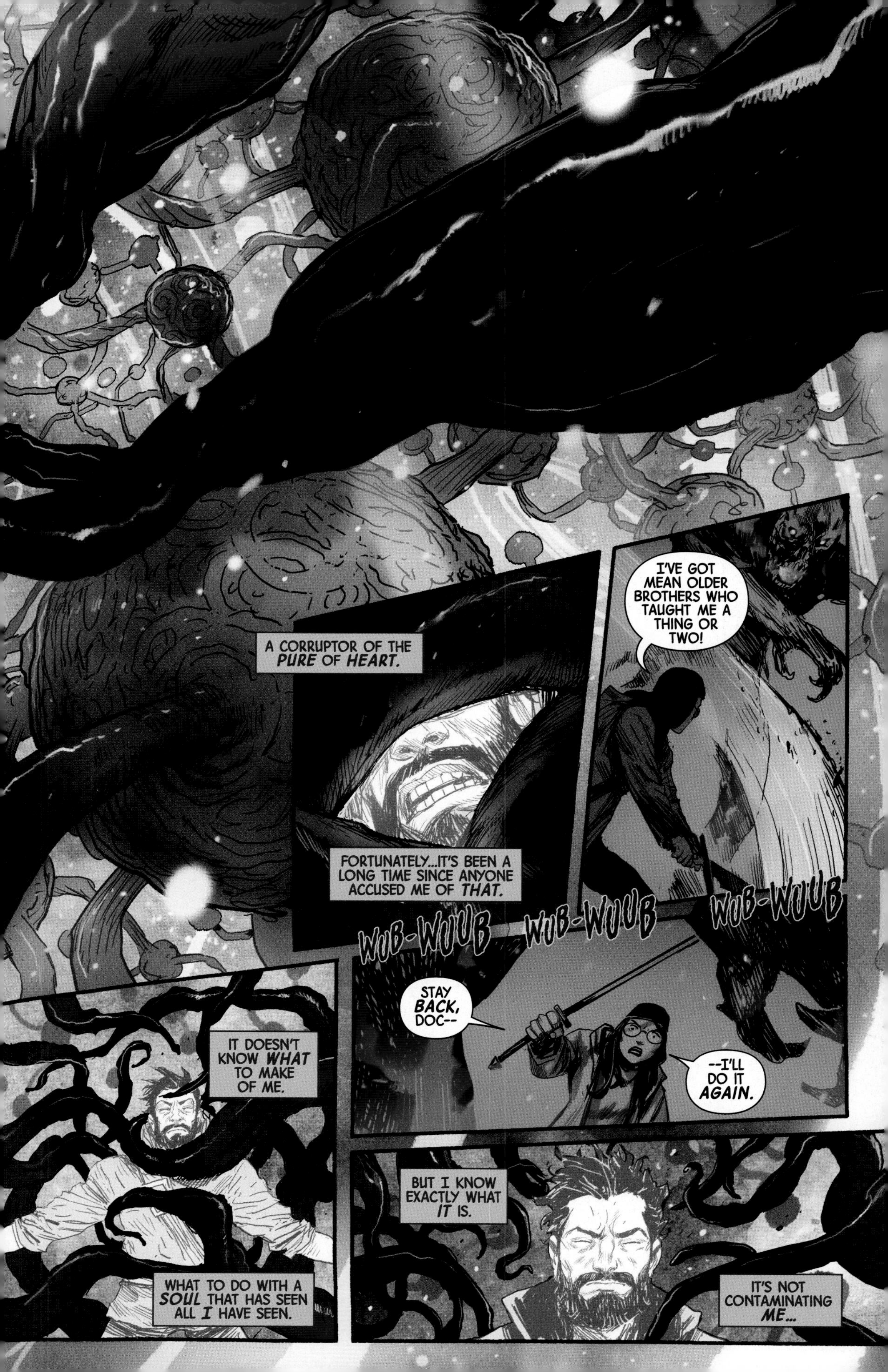
A CORRUPTOR OF THE PURE OF HEART.
FORTUNATELY...IT'S BEEN A LONG TIME SINCE ANYONE ACCUSED ME OF THAT.
I'VE GOT MEAN OLDER BROTHERS WHO TAUGHT ME A THING OR TWO!
WUB-WUUB
WUB-WUUB
WUB-WUUB
IT DOESN'T KNOW WHAT TO MAKE OF ME.
WHAT TO DO WITH A SOUL THAT HAS SEEN ALL I HAVE SEEN.
STAY BACK, DOC--
--I'LL DO IT AGAIN.
BUT I KNOW EXACTLY WHAT IT IS.
IT'S NOT CONTAMINATING ME...

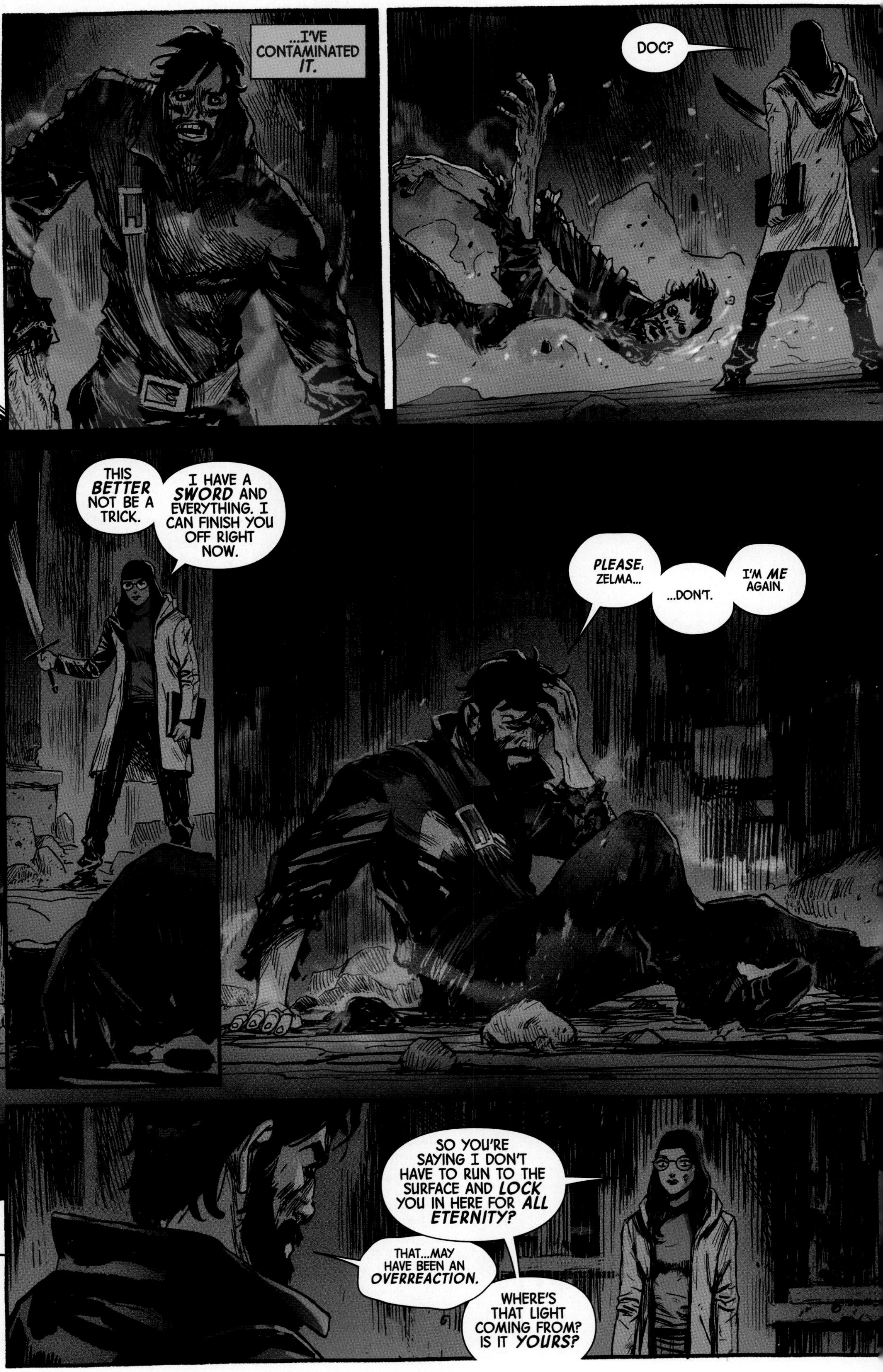
...I'VE CONTAMINATED IT.
DOC?
THIS BETTER NOT BE A TRICK.
I HAVE A SWORD AND EVERYTHING. I CAN FINISH YOU OFF RIGHT NOW.
PLEASE, ZELMA...
...DON'T.
I'M ME AGAIN.
SO YOU'RE SAYING I DON'T HAVE TO RUN TO THE SURFACE AND LOCK YOU IN HERE FOR ALL ETERNITY?
THAT...MAY HAVE BEEN AN OVERREACTION.
WHERE'S THAT LIGHT COMING FROM? IS IT YOURS?

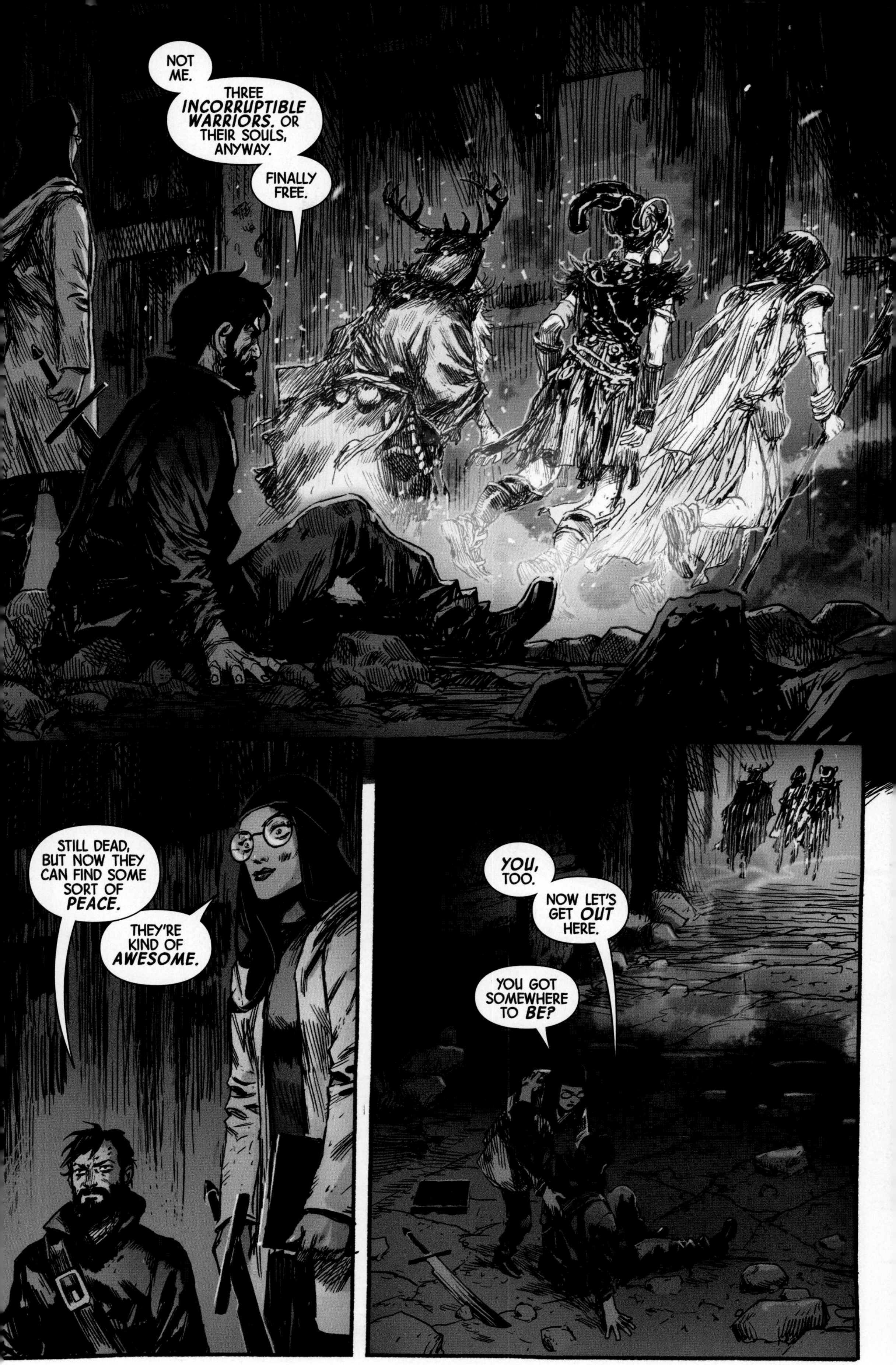
NOT ME.
THREE *INCORRUPTIBLE WARRIORS.* OR THEIR SOULS, ANYWAY.
FINALLY FREE.
STILL DEAD, BUT NOW THEY CAN FIND SOME SORT OF *PEACE.*
THEY'RE KIND OF *AWESOME.*
YOU, TOO.
NOW LET'S GET *OUT* HERE.
YOU GOT SOMEWHERE TO *BE?*

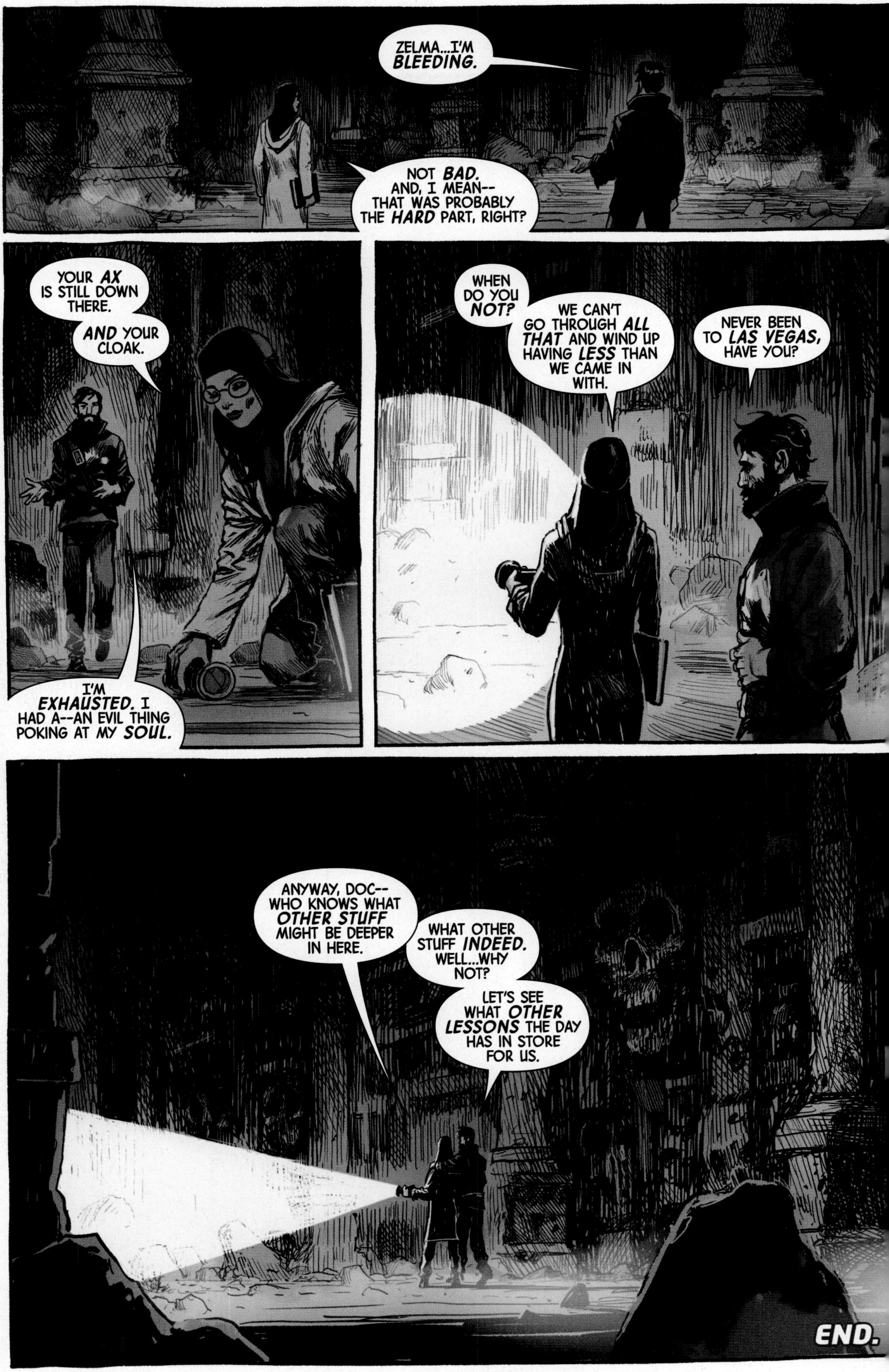
ZELMA...I'M BLEEDING.
NOT BAD. AND, I MEAN-- THAT WAS PROBABLY THE HARD PART, RIGHT?
YOUR AX IS STILL DOWN THERE.
AND YOUR CLOAK.
I'M EXHAUSTED. I HAD A--AN EVIL THING POKING AT MY SOUL.
WHEN DO YOU NOT?
WE CAN'T GO THROUGH ALL THAT AND WIND UP HAVING LESS THAN WE CAME IN WITH.
NEVER BEEN TO LAS VEGAS, HAVE YOU?
ANYWAY, DOC-- WHO KNOWS WHAT OTHER STUFF MIGHT BE DEEPER IN HERE.
WHAT OTHER STUFF INDEED. WELL...WHY NOT?
LET'S SEE WHAT OTHER LESSONS THE DAY HAS IN STORE FOR US.
END.

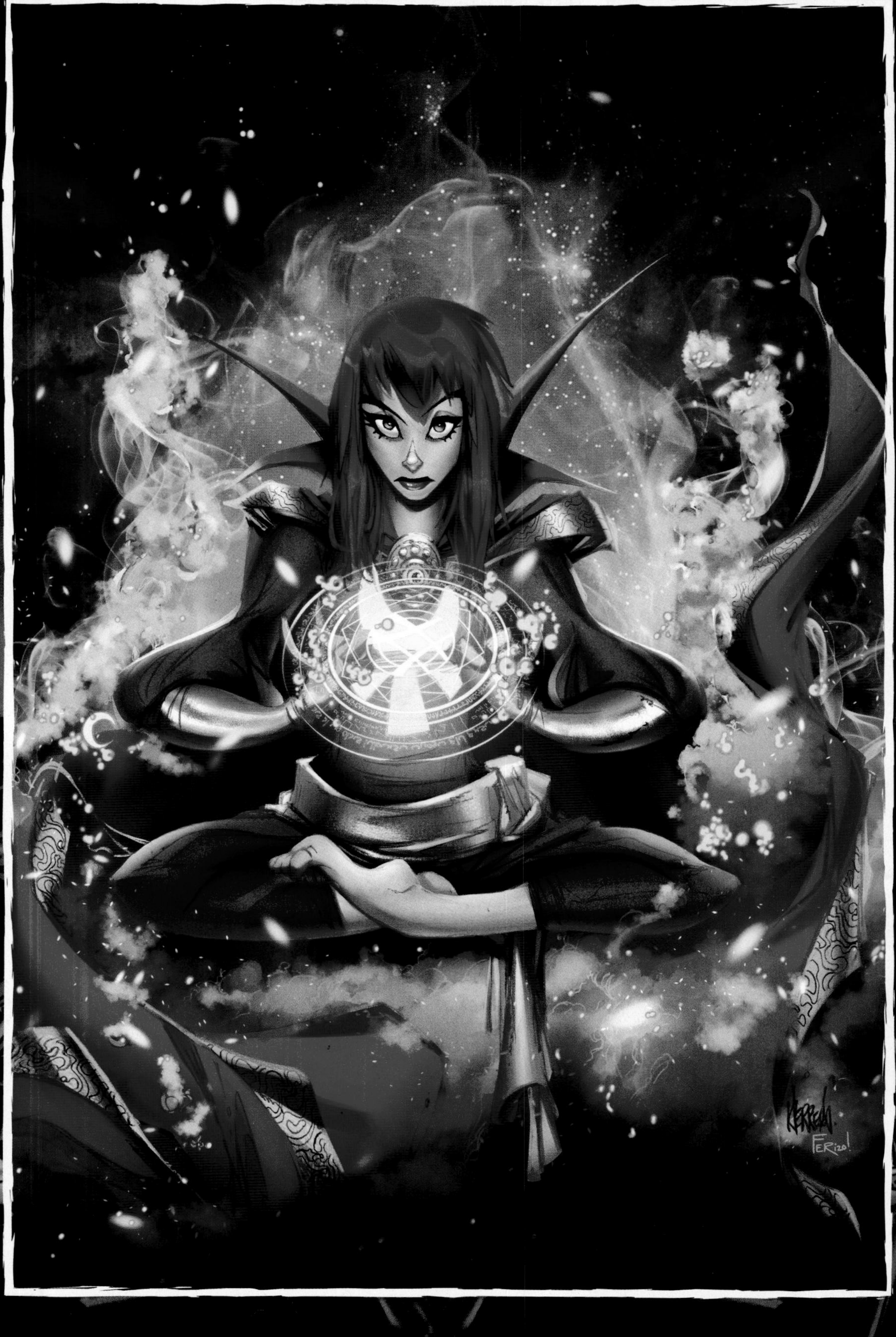

#22 MARY JANE VARIANT BY **FRANCISCO HERRERA** & **FERNANDA RIZO**

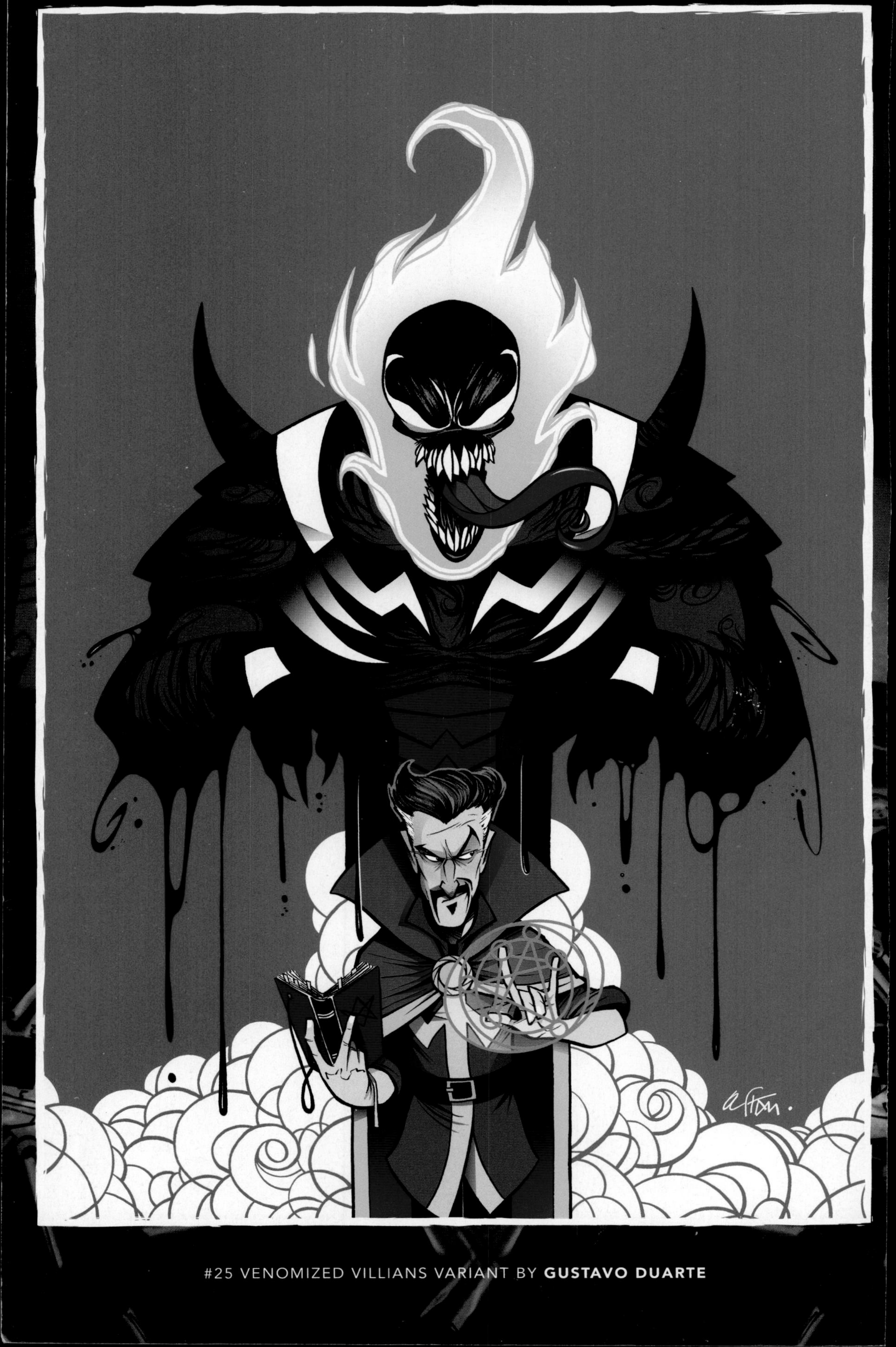

#25 VENOMIZED VILLIANS VARIANT BY **GUSTAVO DUARTE**